MW00585846

"We first met Matt Merker after hearing his incredible hymn, 'He Will Hold Me Fast.' Since then, he has become a friend, cowriter, and eventually, fellow leader in our team. His vision and voice on the subject of the gathered worship of God's people has enriched so much of our thinking personally and in our organization. Matt shows pastors, music leaders, and all of us how to keep our focus on the Bible's priorities for corporate worship: God's glory, the church's growth, and proclaiming the gospel to the world. As Matt himself says, you do not need to agree with every specific application for this volume to be a major help in planning and preparing for the Sunday service. Rather, this book reminds us all to rediscover the wonderful reality that God gathers us together as a united body to hear his word and sing his praise. We have long been praying for a deepening of congregational worship around the globe in the twenty-first century, and we warmly commend this book as one resource that we trust will be used by God toward that end."

Keith and Kristyn Getty, hymn writers; recording artists; authors, *Sing! How Worship Transforms Your Life, Family, and Church*

"The worship of God demands our full attention. It is not a subject to be taken lightly, but thoughtfully and biblically. This contribution by Matt Merker points us in that direction, and anyone charged with leading corporate worship would do well to listen."

Matt Boswell, Pastor, The Trails Church, Celina, Texas; hymn writer

"A number of books in recent decades have addressed the vital topic of what God wants churches to do when they gather on the Lord's day. Some are richly theological. Others are thoughtfully practical. Matt Merker's new book, *Corporate Worship*, is both and more. Drawing from a diverse church background and a deep commitment to studying and applying God's word, Matt stands firm on nonnegotiable issues and winsomely approaches negotiable ones. Above all, he keeps us focused on Jesus Christ, the one in whose name we gather, and whose substitutionary death and victorious resurrection are the reason we worship. Wherever you find yourself on the liturgical spectrum, *Corporate Worship* will encourage you toward more theologically driven, emotionally engaging, and Christ-exalting gatherings."

Bob Kauflin, Director, Sovereign Grace Music; author, *Worship Matters* and *True Worshipers*

"Not too many people have stopped to think about what it means to worship, let alone what it means to worship together as the body of Christ. This brief but significant book will help you understand the nature of corporate worship in a biblical sense. Matt Merker reminds us that we gather together at God's invitation to glorify his name and to celebrate as a community what he has done in and through the work of Christ. The church gathering is only a foretaste of what will take place in heaven, as we can glimpse from Revelation 5. What we do in personal worship should have a corporate expression to reflect the unity of the Spirit and as a testimony to the unbelieving world. Merker is trying to help the worship experience of the church of our days as we understand its nature and the purpose for which we gather."

Miguel Núñez, Senior Pastor, International Baptist Church of Santo Domingo, Dominican Republic

"In this book, Matt Merker brings to us in a refreshing way a truth about the church that we often take for granted: namely, that the church is a gathered community for the purpose of worshiping God. Even under intense, life-threatening persecution, God's people gather together and worship their Creator, Sustainer, Savior, and soon-coming King. This book is about why this must be the case and what ought to happen when the church gathers. Read it to underpin the vital place of corporate worship in your life as a believer and, indeed, in the life of your church!"

Conrad Mbewe, Pastor, Kabwata Baptist Church, Lusaka, Zambia

"When correctly understood, corporate worship is more than just the highlight of the life of the church—it is the very center of the life of the church. When we gather, not only is the health and vitality of the church body put on display, but corporate worship also shapes and strengthens the life of the church. There is simply no way for a church to bypass anemic corporate gatherings to health in the life of the church. This little book is packed with both doctrine and counsel that will help the reader press toward a more Scripture-shaped vision for corporate worship. There is a treasure trove of grace to be found by the saints who will give themselves to approaching God in worship on his terms. In this book you will not only find helpful counsel on ways you can improve your corporate gatherings, but you will also be resourced with the biblical thinking that lies behind the biblical practice we all desire to grow in."

Kenneth Mbugua, Senior Pastor, Emmanuel Baptist Church, Nairobi, Kenya

CORPORATE WORSHIP

9Marks: Building Healthy Churches

Edited by Mark Dever and Jonathan Leeman

Corporate Worship: How the Church Gathers as God's People, Matt Merker (2021)

Deacons: How They Serve and Strengthen the Church, Matt Smethurst (2021)

Prayer: How Praying Together Shapes the Church, John Onwuchekwa (2018)

Biblical Theology: How the Church Faithfully Teaches the Gospel, Nick Roark and Robert Cline (2018)

Missions: How the Local Church Goes Global, Andy Johnson (2017)

Conversion: How God Creates a People, Michael Lawrence (2017)

Discipling: How to Help Others Follow Jesus, Mark Dever (2016)

The Gospel: How the Church Portrays the Beauty of Christ, Ray Ortlund (2014)

Expositional Preaching: How We Speak God's Word Today, David R. Helm (2014)

Evangelism: How the Whole Church Speaks of Jesus, J. Mack Stiles (2014)

Church Elders: How to Shepherd God's People Like Jesus, Jeramie Rinne (2014)

Sound Doctrine: How a Church Grows in the Love and Holiness of God, Bobby Jamieson (2013)

Church Membership: How the World Knows Who Represents Jesus, Jonathan Leeman (2012)

Church Discipline: How the Church Protects the Name of Jesus, Jonathan Leeman (2012)

BUILDING HEALTHY CHURCHES

CORPORATE WORSHIP

HOW
THE CHURCH
GATHERS
AS GOD'S
PEOPLE

MATT MERKER

Foreword by Ligon Duncan

:: CROSSWAY®

WHEATON, ILLINOIS

Cover illustration: Wayne Brezinka

First printing 2021

Printed in the United States of America

Scripture quotations are from the ESV® Bible (The Holy Bible, English Standard Version®), copyright © 2001 by Crossway, a publishing ministry of Good News Publishers. Used by permission. All rights reserved.

All emphases in Scripture quotations have been added by the author.

Hardcover ISBN: 978-1-4335-6982-1
ePub ISBN: 978-1-4335-6985-2
PDF ISBN: 978-1-4335-6983-8
Mobipocket ISBN: 978-1-4335-6984-5

Library of Congress Cataloging-in-Publication Data

Names: Merker, Matt, 1984- author. | Duncan, J. Ligon, 1960- writer of foreword.
Title: Corporate worship : how the church gathers as God's people / Matt Merker ; foreword by Ligon Duncan.
Description: Wheaton, Illinois : Crossway, [2021] | Series: 9Marks : building healthy churches | Includes bibliographical references and index.
Identifiers: LCCN 2020025108 (print) | LCCN 2020025109 (ebook) | ISBN 9781433569821 (hardcover) | ISBN 9781433569838 (pdf) | ISBN 9781433569845 (mobi) | ISBN 9781433569852 (epub)
Subjects: LCSH: Public worship. | Religious gatherings. | Church attendance.
Classification: LCC BV15 .M47 2021 (print) | LCC BV15 (ebook) | DDC 264—dc23
LC record available at https://lccn.loc.gov/2020025108
LC ebook record available at https://lccn.loc.gov/2020025109

Crossway is a publishing ministry of Good News Publishers.

LB		30	29	28	27	26	25	24	23	22	21
15	14	13	12	11	10	9	8	7	6	5	4	3	2	1

For Erica, Lena, and Isaiah

CONTENTS

FOREWORD

This is a book about worship, specifically "corporate worship," that is, believers gathering for the express purpose of giving praise to God. That is a very important subject and activity. People were created, and Christians were redeemed, in order to worship. Paul makes that clear in Ephesians 1, where he says that everything in God's plan of salvation, from before the beginning of time, is meant to lead up to our being "to the praise of his glory." And in case we miss this, he says it three times (Eph. 1:6, 12, and 14). Hughes Oliphant Old (who probably knew more about the history of Christian worship than any other Protestant writer in recent times) points us to the Psalms and then back to this passage in Paul to explain:

> We worship God because God created us to worship him. Worship is at the center of our existence, at the heart of our reason for being. God created us to be his image—an image that would reflect his glory. In fact, the whole creation was brought into existence to reflect the divine glory. The psalmist tells us that "the heavens are telling the glory of God; and the firmament proclaims his handiwork" (Ps. 19:1). The apostle Paul in the prayer with which he begins the epistle to the Ephesians makes it clear that God created us to praise him:

> Blessed be the God and Father of our Lord Jesus
> Christ, who has blessed us in Christ with every spiri-
> tual blessing in the heavenly places, even as he chose
> us in him before the foundation of the world, that
> we should be holy and blameless before him. He des-
> tined us in love to be his sons through Jesus Christ,
> according to the purpose of his will, to the praise of
> his glorious grace . . . (Eph. 1:3–6)

> This prayer says much about the worship of the earliest
> Christians. It shows the consciousness that the first Christians
> had of the ultimate significance of their worship. They under-
> stood themselves to have been destined and appointed to live
> to the praise of God's glory (Eph. 1:12).[1]

What is worship? Well, the psalmist tells us succinctly. It is
giving unto the Lord the glory due his name (Ps. 29:1–2). What,
then, should we aim to do in corporate worship? Our aim, as the
congregation gathers to meet with God in public worship on the
Lord's Day, is to glorify and enjoy God, in accordance with his
written Word. That is, the very purpose of assembling together
as the people of God in congregational worship is to give to the
Lord the glory due his name and to enjoy the blessing of his
promised special presence with his own people, in obedience
to his instructions set forth in the Scriptures.

Corporate worship (so-called because the body or *corpus*
of Christ, that is, the people of God, the church, is collectively
involved in this encounter with God) is sometimes referred
to as "gathered," "assembled," "public," or "congregational"

---

[1] Hughes Oliphant Old, *Worship: Reformed according to Scripture* (Louisville: Westminster/
John Knox, 2002), 1.

worship. All of these names are helpful, and bring out different dimensions of this important aspect of biblical worship. Though the Bible indicates that there are, in addition to public worship, other distinct and significant facets of Christian worship (like family worship, private worship, and worship in all of life), the importance of public or corporate worship is featured in both the Old and New Testaments. When Psalm 100:2 and Hebrews 10:25 speak of "coming before the Lord" and "assembling together" they are both addressing public or gathered worship.

As Christians, we believe it is important that we worship corporately, for God has made us his family, and corporate worship is a family meeting with God. It is the covenant community engaging with God, gathering with his people to seek his face, to glorify and enjoy him, to hear his Word, to revel in the glory of union and communion with him, to respond to his Word, to render praise back to him, to give unto him the glory due his name.

The New Testament makes clear that the congregation of Christians, this family, this body, this community, is the place where God is especially present in this world. In the days of the old covenant, the place where God manifested his special presence was "the tabernacle" or "the temple" or "Jerusalem." In the new covenant, that special "place" is now wherever the Lord's house, that is, his people, is gathered. Jesus stresses this to the Samaritan woman (John 4:21) and to his disciples in addressing congregational discipline (Matt. 18:20, surely a solemn component of the life of the gathered church). The place of new covenant worship is no longer inextricably tied to a geographical location and a physical structure but to a gathered people. This is why, in the old Scottish tradition, as the people gathered to enter a church building, it would be said that "the Kirk[2] goes in" rather than, as we often say, "we are going to church." The new covenant *locus* or place of the special presence of God with the church militant is in this gathered body, wherever it might be—whether in catacombs, or a storefront, or a beautiful colonial church building. This makes corporate worship extremely important.

The great distinctive of the whole approach to public worship commended in this book is that we aim for the form and substance of our corporate worship to be biblical, to be suffused with and guided by Scripture and scriptural theology. An apt motto for this approach is, "Read the Bible, Preach the Bible, Pray the Bible, Sing the Bible, See the Bible (visibly depicted in the ordinances of Baptism and the Lord's Supper)."

As a pastor, I am always looking for sound Christian writers who can help me explain these kinds of true, good, and important things better—more simply, scripturally, clearly, and compellingly. Matt Merker helps me do precisely that in this book. I lost count of the times I thought to myself, "that is really well put. That helps my own soul, and I can use that biblical truth, articulated in that way, to better equip the saints in their public praise of God." But he also helps me diagnose some unique current challenges to my people in their understanding and practice of congregational worship. Two (among others) stand out to me.

---

[2] The Scots word for "church."

Matt mentions what has been called "liturgical pragmatism," that is, a decision to do "whatever works" to reach out to and evangelize unbelievers. I think that approach has effectively de-churched many churches in my lifetime, and left generations of Christians with a lack of understanding of what is supposed to be entailed in Christian corporate worship. This challenge is not the fault of the people but of often-well-meaning pastors and leaders, who want to reach out with the gospel to unbelievers. They sincerely desire to "church the unchurched," but they end up "unchurching the church." Because of their evangelistic pragmatism, their services do not follow biblical patterns and principles and often are bereft of biblical content. Not surprisingly, discipleship and corporate worship suffer in such settings. I think Matt is right in putting his finger on that as a key problem in our time (and sadly, it does continue to be a problem). Over the course of my seventeen years at First Presbyterian Church in Jackson, I had droves of Christian young people join our congregation precisely because they were refugees from these kinds of settings. They were looking for both sound biblical exposition and solid biblical corporate worship.

Another significant problem Matt mentions is that of a consumer mindset. This is a problem of the people (exacerbated by pastors and leaders who play to it). If we come as religious consumers to public services of worship, we will have the attitude of a customer, and the customer, as they say, is always right. It's all about what we want, what we think, about our opinion. So we ask, *Did I like the musicians and the music?* rather than, did the congregational singing help me worship

God and was it filled with the truth of Scripture? We ask, *Did I like the preacher and his preaching?* rather than, was the preaching faithful to the Bible, and did it expound God, the gospel, and godliness from his Word, and did I respond to it in faith, wonder, love, and praise of God? C. S. Lewis has Screwtape advise his demon understudy Wormwood that if he can't cure a man of churchgoing he should aim to turn him into a taster or connoisseur of churches: "the search for a 'suitable' church makes the man a critic where the Enemy wants him to be a pupil."[3]

If we think of ourselves as consumers, we will view ourselves as the audience, and the preacher and others assisting in leading the service (especially the musicians) as performers there to inspire (and perhaps entertain) us, rather than understanding that God is the audience and we are beggars, rebels, and enemies, made heirs, friends, and children of God through the Father's love, the Son's obedience, death, and resurrection, and the Spirit's new birth, and that we have come now, by his grace, to give something to God that he alone deserves and that we can only give him through Jesus Christ, in order that we might be what he made us to be (worshipers) and enjoy what he made us to enjoy: the greatest, deepest, best treasure in all the world (the triune God himself, and communion with him).

So, this is all to say that Matt Merker helps both pastors and people think biblically about congregational worship. He asks us to think about who exactly it is that gathers to worship, the necessity of that gathering, the purpose of our gathering

---

[3] C. S. Lewis, *Screwtape Letters* (New York: Macmillan, 1942), 81–82.

(and I loved his threefold consideration of exaltation, edification, and evangelism in that chapter), the content or substance of our gathered worship, the order or structure of our gathering, and our participation in the gathering.

I think you will be helped, as I was, in reading this little book. You may well read it in one sitting, but I believe that you will return to it again, as I already have, and plan to do in days ahead, God willing.

Ligon Duncan
Chancellor/CEO of Reformed Theological Seminary
John E. Richards Professor of Systematic and Historical Theology

SERIES PREFACE

Do you believe it's your responsibility to help build a healthy church? If you are a Christian, we believe that it is.

Jesus commands you to make disciples (Matt. 28:18–20). Jude says to build yourselves up in the faith (Jude 20–21). Peter calls you to use your gifts to serve others (1 Pet. 4:10). Paul tells you to speak the truth in love so that your church will become mature (Eph. 4:13, 15). Do you see where we are getting this?

Whether you are a church member or leader, the Building Healthy Churches series of books aims to help you fulfill such biblical commands and so play your part in building a healthy church. Another way to say it might be, we hope these books will help you grow in loving your church like Jesus loves your church.

In this series, 9Marks has produced short, readable books on each of what Mark has called nine marks of a healthy church—plus a few more. These include books on expositional preaching, biblical theology, sound doctrine, the gospel, conversion, evangelism, church membership, church discipline, discipleship and growth, church elders, deacons, prayer, missions, and corporate worship.

Local churches exist to display God's glory to the nations. We do that by fixing our eyes on the gospel of Jesus Christ, trusting him for salvation, and then loving one another with God's own holiness, unity, and love. We pray the book you are holding will help.

With hope,
Mark Dever and Jonathan Leeman
series editors

SPECIAL THANKS

Thanks are due, first of all, to Capitol Hill Baptist Church. Thank you for all that you taught me about corporate worship by gathering each Lord's Day. I'm grateful to all the elders and members for how you loved, taught, supported, and cared for my family and me for a decade. Thanks to Bobby Jamieson, who encouraged me to pursue this project, rearranged my schedule to help me write, and offered input on the manuscript. And particular thanks to Mark Dever for the investment you have made and continue to make in my life. Your influence permeates this whole book.

Thank you to the wonderful 9Marks staff for your commitment to building healthy churches and for your expert support. Alex Duke transformed this book with his superb editing. Special thanks to Jonathan Leeman for shepherding my initial idea into a completed volume, with lots of advice and improvement along the way.

Thank you to Crossway for your commitment to equipping the broader church with biblical resources and for allowing me to add a contribution to this 9Marks series.

Thanks to the many friends who read part or all of the manuscript and offered valuable feedback: Isaac Adams, Sam Emadi, Amos Evans, Susanna Farmer, Jennifer Gosselin, Drew

Hodge, Dave Hunt, Jonny Lim, Matthias Lohmann, Tony Merritt, Jonathan Morgan, Leandro Pasquini, Shanyl Philip, John Sarver, and Shane Williamson. I'm especially grateful to Devon Kauflin, who spent several long lunches talking through various chapters and sharing from his deep wells of wisdom.

Finally, thank you to my kind and precious family. I love you, and this book is for you. Erica, your delight in worshiping Christ fuels my own. Lena and Isaiah, I pray that Christ would become precious to you, and that you would join the sacred assembly that ever sings his praise.

INTRODUCTION

My mother shook a tambourine. My younger siblings rattled maracas. My hands played a few simple chords on an out-of-tune piano. Together we sang, "Celebrate Jesus, celebrate!"

That's how every day at Merker Home School Academy began: with "worship."

I've been around church music my whole life. In the Vineyard church in which I grew up, we sang simple choruses of devotion. Then, in the Conservative Baptist church of my teenage years, I found myself unwittingly enlisted in a "worship war": the organ against the praise band. The band won. This stylistic transition was painful, and quite commonplace in the 1990s. In college, I grew to love hymns both old and new that coupled deep truths with singable melodies. After graduation, I returned to the church of my youth and reenlisted in that praise band.

For decades, I sang to Jesus at home and at Sunday services. I listened to "praise and worship" albums. I led worship services at youth groups, college fellowships, and even vocationally at church.

And yet, I didn't understand corporate worship.

Then, at twenty-four, I began a pastoral internship. For the first time, I studied what the Bible says about the local church. What I found changed me forever. No longer did I regard the church as an optional add-on to the Christian faith, or a place where "really serious" believers got together to grow, or a rally designed to attract outsiders through inspiring experience. The church is the bride for whom Christ died. It is the outpost of his kingdom on earth. It is the temple for his Spirit. It is his body. I recognized these images beforehand, to be sure. But now I started to put them together. I saw they have rich implications for what a church does when it meets.

At the same time, I participated in church gatherings every Sunday that were deeply and deliberately congregational. The whole church wanted to be there. Everyone engaged intently. Folks stayed afterwards for an hour to minister to one another. And the whole church *sang*—more loudly and passionately than I'd ever heard, even though the musical accompaniment was plain and unremarkable.

I realized there's a connection between how a congregation understands itself to *be* a church, and the way it worships *as* a church.

Needless to say, I stayed around for a while. I made that church, Capitol Hill Baptist Church in Washington, DC, my home for a decade. God used its congregational life—including the worship services I've just described—to grow my faith by leaps and bounds.

Why another book on worship? I've been asked that question several times. Each time, my answer has been the same: this isn't a book on worship in general. It's about *corporate* worship.

To be sure, worship by itself is a worthy topic. We're created to be worshipers of God. There is no one Hebrew word in the Old Testament or one Greek word in the New Testament that translates exclusively as "worship," because the idea is so pervasive. Scripture calls all people to love, serve, obey, exalt, magnify, sing to, ascribe worth to, and bow down before the one true God. Worship, simply put, is the purpose of life. It is "an engagement with [God] on the terms that he proposes and in the way that he alone makes possible."[1] Because Christ offered himself for us, believers now offer him our whole lives—all we think, do, and say—as a worshipful sacrifice (Rom. 12:1).

That's not all, though. A life of worship also involves assembling with God's people. The New Testament commands believers to meet together (Heb. 10:24–25) and gives whole chapters of instruction pertinent to these gatherings (e.g., 1 Corinthians 11–14). A church service is different than when several people who all happen to be Christians get together to play sports or watch a movie. Scripture teaches that there is a time "when you come together *as a church*" (1 Cor. 11:18). The whole gathering is "worship," not just the singing and music. In the preaching, prayers, and everything in between, God ministers to and through the whole congregation for his own glory.

That gathering, that "coming together" of the church, is what this book is about.

My goal is simple. I hope to show that in order to understand corporate worship, we must understand the local church. When we approach the Sunday service with a biblical

---

[1] David Peterson, *Engaging with God: A Biblical Theology of Worship* (Downers Grove, IL: IVP Academic, 1992), 20.

view of the church body, it transforms how we engage in gathered worship. My aim is to put the "corporate" into our corporate worship.

Why does this topic matter? Imagine a group of Christians who are planting a church. Their conversation turns to their hopes and dreams for the Sunday worship gathering.

Brad says that what their church needs is *intimate corporate worship*. He highlights passionate communion with Jesus. "That's authentic worship," he says, "when the Spirit brings us to the throne room in awe and adoration."

Alyssa tells Brad to beware too much focus on personal experience. After all, the Bible calls us to *historic, doctrinal corporate worship*. "We should herald the truth while showing our solidarity with Christians of past generations through ancient creeds and classic hymns."

Rich agrees with Alyssa to an extent, but he urges his friends to focus on *liturgical corporate worship*. Yes, intimacy and truth both matter, he says, but, when we worship, God forms believers through embodied practices. "We're physical beings, so we must appreciate how liturgy shapes our desires, how the rituals of the body train the posture of the heart."

Danielle throws up her hands in frustration. "Guys! Everything you're talking about sounds so foreign to unbelievers!" She argues for *outreach-driven corporate worship*. Get rid of the smells, bells, and creeds. Let's play songs our neighbors know, make everything as accessible as possible, and above all, keep the service under an hour.

When we consider how a church should worship, it isn't always exactly clear which of the above perspectives should rank highest. No wonder Christians have argued about corporate worship over the generations. Different believers have different priorities, and our varying theological backgrounds and church traditions point us in various directions.

But much of this confusion can be cleared up if we simply *begin with the local church*. What is a church? What does God's Word call churches to do when they gather? Those are the central questions driving this book. As we answer them, we'll find that the four statements above each have a grain of truth. Corporate worship *does* involve communion with Christ by his Spirit, *and* heralding sound doctrine while staying historically rooted, *and* liturgical formation, *and* serving as a witness to the lost. My purpose isn't to identify any of those sound bites as the "correct" one. Rather, it's to show how a deep understanding of the church brings clarity to this conversation.

Here's how we'll get there. First, a biblical view of the church tells us *who* gathers. The nature of the local church shapes what it does when it meets (chapter 1). A biblical understanding of the church also helps us see that churches *must* gather, and that God is the one who gathers us to work in our midst (chapter 2). It then teaches us *why* we gather: unto God's glory, for our mutual good, before the world's gaze (chapter 3).

Then, a biblical view of the local church informs all the practical aspects of putting a worship service together. Our doctrine of the church helps us answer the questions of what we should do when we gather (chapter 4), how we should order the gathering (chapter 5), and what it looks like for the whole church to participate in every element of corporate worship (chapters 6–7).

You'll notice that I refer a lot to my church in this book. That's because the Lord's Day gatherings at Capitol Hill Baptist Church (CHBC) I've witnessed have sought to fulfill the biblical vision for corporate worship. The church isn't perfect, but it's where I've seen so much about worship faithfully taught and applied.

I'm not encouraging you to make a carbon copy of the corporate worship at CHBC. Corporate worship will look different wherever it takes place. Yet the Bible does address the topic. So I'll seek to talk about core biblical elements of gathered worship that should be present everywhere, even while I also talk about the forms those elements take at CHBC. My hope is that you would glean from CHBC's example as you try to apply the elements of corporate worship faithfully, in the forms that are wisest for your own context. The forms are flexible; the real question I hope this book helps you answer is, *how does our understanding of the church shape how we seek to fulfill the biblical elements of congregational worship?*

Before I finished this book, the Lord saw fit to move my family and me to Nashville, Tennessee, where I'm now working for a Christian organization that publishes hymns and educational material on worship. We've joined a local congregation, Edgefield Church, that gathers for wonderful, Christ-centered corporate services. But most of this book was already done when we moved. So when I refer to "my church" in this book, it's still CHBC I'm talking about. It was through the beloved brothers and sisters of that congregation that the Lord taught me so many invaluable lessons about corporate worship. Their fingerprints are all over this volume.

Finally, who is this book for? It is for Christians. This topic should matter particularly to those involved in planning and leading church gatherings, from pastors and worship leaders to choir directors and musical volunteers. But at the end of the day, as I hope to stress, corporate worship is the responsibility of every church member. Being a believer means gathering with God's people, for God's praise.

So whoever you are, and whatever your role is in the weekly service, I pray that this brief volume will help you connect what the church *is* to what it *does* in corporate worship.

1

WHO GATHERS?

Dinnertime is a big deal in my family. It's the main time each day when we pause from all the work, chores, ballet practice, and crayons to focus on one another.

On the surface, our meal probably looks like the one enjoyed by millions of families. But if you watched us, you would notice a few distinct things that make us Merkers— that express our "Merkerness." For instance, we are believers in Jesus, so we pray and thank God for the food. My wife is Italian-American, so we often eat the most amazing pasta that you've ever tasted. You would notice the inside jokes, the unspoken rules, the family traditions, and the silly antics that make us *us*.

Who we are as a family shapes what we do. Then what we *do* when we gather around the family table shapes who we are. Our meal flows from and reinforces our family identity.

It's different when I eat dinner alone. If the rest of my family is sick or away on a trip, I can consume the same nutrients while watching television and listening to heavy metal. There are fewer dishes and spilled peas to clean up. But—and it's an important "but"—I don't come away with the same wonderful afterglow. The meal may feed my belly, but it doesn't bind me to the people I love most.

My hope in this book is to show that worshiping God together as a church is like a family dinner. It's an essentially corporate thing. Christians are called to offer God our whole individual lives as worshipful sacrifices (Rom. 12:1). But when we gather as a congregation, something unique happens: we enjoy Christ, exalt God, and edify one another together as his covenant people.

The whole is more than the sum of the parts.

The nature of the church shapes what corporate worship is. The church's worship, in turn, forms and reinforces our corporate identity. So, in order to understand worship, we need to understand the local church.

Many conversations about worship treat the *how* questions. How do we contextualize? What style of music should we use? Organ or rock band? How loud should the speakers be? These aren't unimportant questions, but if they're the main focus, we'll miss something crucial. The more fundamental question is a *who* question: who is worshiping?[1] Our ecclesiology (our doctrine of the church) and our doxology (our doctrine of worship) shape and reinforce one another.

---

[1] Of course, there is another vital *who* question: Whom do Christians worship? The answer is the triune God, our Creator and Redeemer, who has revealed himself to us in Jesus Christ. To understand worship, we must know the one true God. Thankfully, many books on worship stress God-centeredness. I'm going to focus on the other *who* question, the question of who's doing the worshiping, because I think it's relatively underappreciated today. For more on the importance of theology proper (the doctrine of God) in worship, see, e.g., Bob Kauflin, *Worship Matters: Leading Others to Encounter the Greatness of God* (Wheaton, IL: Crossway, 2008), 61–87; D. A. Carson, "Worship under the Word," in *Worship By the Book*, ed. D. A. Carson (Grand Rapids, MI: Zondervan, 2002), 26–33; Michael Lawrence and Mark Dever, "Blended Worship," in *Perspectives on Christian Worship: Five Views*, ed. J. Matthew Pinson (Nashville: B&H Academic, 2009), 226–230.

As with my family meals, who we are as a church shapes our gatherings, and our gatherings shape who we are.

THE CORPORATE NATURE OF SALVATION

God has always related to his people not only as individuals but also as a corporate body. In Genesis, he calls both Abraham and his family. In Exodus, he rescues this family, Israel, and makes them "a kingdom of priests and a holy nation" (Ex. 19:6). What do priests do? They worship. They mediate God's presence and consecrate what's holy. By calling the whole people a "kingdom of priests," God gave them a priestly commission—to be a worshiping, mediating, consecrated people.

The rest of the Old Testament is the history of this nation set apart for God's glory. Though God would ultimately hold each Israelite responsible for his or her own sin (Ezek. 18:1–20), he dealt with them as a people knit together by his covenant.

It's no surprise, then, that when Jesus arrives on the scene, he highlights the corporate nature of the people he came to save. "I will build my *church*," he says (Matt. 16:18). He tells his followers to "*gather* in my name" (Matt. 18:20). Paul affirms that Jesus "died for *us*" (Rom. 5:8; 1 Thess. 5:10). Christ "loved the *church* and gave himself up for her" (Eph. 5:25).

Ephesians 2 is one of the places where Scripture most clearly emphasizes the corporate nature of our salvation. Verses 1 to 10 famously describe how God gives new life by grace to those who trust in Jesus. He reconciles us to himself vertically. But verses 11 to 22 tell the second half of the story, which involves a horizontal reconciliation. Not only were we dead in sins and deserving of God's righteous condemnation, we were also "strangers," "alienated" from God's covenant people (vv. 12–13). The good news? "But now in Christ Jesus you who once were far off have been brought near by the blood of Christ." And the result in verse 19 is corporate: "So then you are no longer strangers and aliens, but you are fellow citizens with the saints and members of the household of God."

A sinner who repents and trusts in Christ isn't only born again. He's born into a new family. The horizontal follows the vertical.

Peter teaches us the same thing. He makes the receiving of God's mercy parallel with becoming a people, as seen when we reset the verse in poetic format:

> Once you were not a people, but now you are God's people;
> once you had not received mercy, but now you have received mercy. (1 Pet. 2:10)

The two things happen together.

This people, this family, becomes visible today in local churches. Though all believers in all times belong to the heavenly "assembly" of the universal church (Heb. 12:23), Jesus established the local church to show the world who his worshipers are.

That should lead us to ask, what is a church? The early Protestant Reformers answered by pointing to a congregation gathered for the right preaching of the gospel and the proper administration of baptism and the Lord's Supper. The early Baptists emphasized the "mutual agreement" or covenant among those gathered. Here's how I would summarize: A local church is an assembly of blood-bought, Spirit-filled worshipers who build one another up by God's Word and affirm one another as citizens of Christ's kingdom through the ordinances.

This means that being a Christian—a worshiper of God—entails identifying with God's worshiping people. You've been adopted into his family. So when you sit down to the dinner table of corporate worship, you don't do so alone. Since salvation is corporate, worship is corporate.

PORTRAITS OF THE CHURCH

So what is the biblical vision for the church, and how does it inform our understanding of corporate worship? Let's consider three biblical images for the church.[2]

An Outpost of the Kingdom of Heaven

First, a local church is an outpost of the kingdom of heaven. This image teaches that our corporate worship should demonstrate how we are distinct from the world.

I once rode my bike near RFK Stadium in Washington, DC, during a soccer game. One of the teams was from Honduras, and hundreds of their tailgating fans filled the parking lot. Flags flew. Music blasted. Meat sizzled on the grill. It wasn't an official Honduran outpost, but it seemed that way: a beautifully distinct group of people on foreign soil. I both felt like an

---

[2] The Bible contains many images or metaphors for the church. I am focusing on these three because they are especially prominent. For more, see D. J. Tidball, "Church," in *New Dictionary of Biblical Theology*, ed. T. Desmond Alexander et al. (Downers Grove, IL: InterVarsity Press, 2000), 410.

outsider *and* was attracted to their gathering. I wanted to learn more about their culture (and food!).

In a similar way, a church service is a gathering of "exiles" who belong to the same heavenly country (1 Pet. 1:1). My own congregation consists of people from the United States, Brazil, China, the Dominican Republic, Ethiopia, and more. But the New Testament says we are, most fundamentally, "fellow citizens" (Eph. 2:19) of Christ's "holy nation" (1 Pet. 2:9).

In the Old Testament, Israel served as an outpost of God's rule. Now, the church occupies that role. We are Christ's ambassadors (2 Cor. 5:20). He identifies himself with us when we gather in his name (Matt. 18:20). A local congregation is a collection of former outcasts whom the King has justified, brought under his lordship, and empowered to follow his law of justice and love.

This means that a church is a preview of the coming new creation, a "time machine from the future."[3] If you want to see what the society of the redeemed will look like in the new heaven and new earth, you don't need to look farther than any true church. Visit, for instance, my friend Joshua's house church in China. Or Faith Baptist Church in Kitwe, Zambia. Or St. Helen's Bishopsgate, an Anglican church in London. A church is a movie trailer—albeit a flawed and imperfect one—for what God's kingdom on earth will look like on the final day.

What does this mean for corporate worship? Here are several implications:

---

[3] Jonathan Leeman, "We Come in Peace: Churches, Time-Machines and a Gospel Apologetic," *Primer* 7 (November 2018): 46.

- *We gather as ambassadors, not consumers.* The goal of a worship service is not to entertain or to provide an inspiring experience. It is to honor our King and make him known.
- *We don't "go to church" to worship; we worship because we are the church.* If we treat church merely as an event to attend, we're more likely to slip into a self-centered mindset. We'll rate a service based on how it served us. Yet the Scriptures we've considered show that belonging to a local church is integral to the Christian life. We join and gather because it's who we are. When we worship, we embody—make visible in space and time—our distinct corporate identity.
- *Everything we do in worship should submit to Scripture.* Ambassadors don't set government policy. They faithfully apply it. Similarly, we don't write the script for what to do in a church meeting. We obey the orders our King has given us in his Word.
- *A worship gathering is where we declare heaven's judgments.* Just as an ambassador speaks on behalf of his or her country, the church serves as the mouthpiece for God's kingdom. This isn't just true of our sermons. When we confess our sin in corporate prayer, we tell the world that we assent to God's verdict against us. When we sing a song of praise, we tell the world that we agree with the Father's delight in his Son.
- *When we worship, we exemplify the culture of God's kingdom.* A church is countercultural. Its worship services should be so too. After all, our meetings are like a gathering of exiles on foreign soil. We declare our pledge of allegiance in the creed. We sing our national anthem in the hymns. We teach our constitution in the preaching of the Word. We issue passports (that is, we identify believers as belonging to Christ's kingdom) when we baptize. And we enjoy a foretaste of our future national feast when we take the Lord's Supper. In all

these ways, we "disrupt" the prevailing culture of our age and disciple believers in the culture of the King.[4]

- *Our worship services should be evangelistic.* Although we shouldn't cater our meetings to the whims of unbelievers, we should pray that they would attend (1 Cor. 14:24). The gathering should beckon—even command—citizens of the domain of darkness to defect to the kingdom of light: "We implore you on behalf of Christ, be reconciled to God" (2 Cor. 5:20).

To sum it all up: since the church is a foretaste of the new Jerusalem, our worship should exhibit our distinct nationality and the pleasant aroma of heaven. It should focus supremely on Jesus, heaven's King. It should embody kingdom priorities. Then, as we worship in this way, God further forms us into more faithful subjects under his rule.

A Holy Temple

Second, a local church is a holy temple. The lesson? In our worship we enjoy direct fellowship with God and one another.

God, of course, is omnipresent. He's everywhere (1 Kings 8:27; Ps. 139:7–10).

Yet at every stage in the storyline of the Bible, God makes his presence specially manifest among his people. He did this first in the garden—the earth's original temple. Then in the tabernacle in the wilderness. Then in Israel's temple. Then in the most perfect temple, his Son. And finally, in all those

---

[4] For the idea that the elements of a worship service are "disruptive" to our culture's prevailing norms, I'm indebted to Alan Noble, *Disruptive Witness: Speaking Truth in a Distracted Age* (Downers Grove, IL: InterVarsity Press, 2018), 133–146.

united to his Son. Paul affirms that each one of our individual bodies is a temple of the Spirit (1 Cor. 6:19), but he also teaches that we are that temple collectively: "Do you not know that you [plural] are God's temple and that God's Spirit dwells in you?" (1 Cor. 3:16; see also Eph 2:22; 1 Pet. 2:5).

Imagine that. God delighted to manifest his special covenant presence in the flawed, messy churches of the New Testament. Amazingly, he does the same among us today.

I was a music major in college. One day, the administration emailed to say there would be an "open rehearsal," and music students were welcome to attend. Who was rehearsing? Oh, no big deal—only Béla Fleck (one of the best banjo players in the world) and Edgar Meyer (one of the best bassists in the world).

We all rushed to the rehearsal hall to hear these musical giants. The atmosphere was totally different than usual. Instead of a mess of instruments, sheet music, and backpacks, we found neat rows of chairs. Instead of chattering noisily, we waited in hushed silence. Why? Because of the presence of greatness.

Their presence had an effect on our relationships as well. "You're a fan, too?" students asked one another. Petty rivalries vanished as the atmosphere grew more festive. For two hours, we were all best friends—united by the presence of two figures we revered.

When the church gathers, we encounter the presence of someone far greater than any musician. Like that rehearsal I attended, the presence of Greatness transforms the relationships of those who are there. Spirit-filled people set aside their worldly differences to worship together as family, "with one voice" (Rom. 15:6).

What does this mean for corporate worship? We can draw several lessons:

- *God's dwelling place has a congregational shape.* If we hope to encounter God's presence when we come to church, we ought to expect to find him in and with one another, rather than primarily in our own personal feelings and intuitions. A church service isn't mainly the place for me to have a souped-up, private "quiet time." It's the place for me to meet God by meeting with his Spirit-filled people.
- *Corporate worship must never be anonymous.* If we are God's temple, then a Christian service is, by definition, a communal affair. Unlike going to a movie, where you try not to notice who is sitting next to you, at church we warmly greet one another because we share the same Spirit. We hear the voices of brothers and sisters we know by name as songs, prayers, and Scriptures reverberate around us. Rather than slipping out of our seats to leave during the final song, we stick around for fellowship. Those whom the world divides by ethnicity, class, or nationality unite together with a holy kiss (Rom. 16:16)—or at least a holy side-hug!
- *Corporate worship is priestly ministry to other believers.* Peter writes, "You yourselves like living stones are being built up as a spiritual house, to be a holy priesthood, to offer spiritual sacrifices acceptable to God through Jesus Christ" (1 Pet. 2:5). When we gather for worship, we all play a priestly role. We offer two types of sacrifice: praise to God (Heb. 13:15); and good works to bless God's people (Heb. 13:16). We minister both vertically to the Lord and horizontally to one another when the church gathers.
- *The real "action" is in the pew, not on the platform (which we often wrongly think of as a "stage").* We should be grate-

ful for everyone whom God equips to facilitate our public worship. They are Spirit-filled priests. But so are we. I fear that too often evangelicals view the church as a place where the worship on a "stage" washes over the rest of us like an emotional force field. It's as if we want to replicate a concert venue, or like we're after the experience of a Roman Catholic mass, where sacramental grace flows down to the people from the altar, via the priests. Yet that's not how we should view a church's worship service. Since we are God's temple, church members already enjoy union with Christ and one another by his Spirit. The pew is the platform. We are a kingdom of priests offering praise to our God, through the sole mediation of Christ.

In our corporate worship, we enjoy fellowship with God and one another. And as we worship, God's Spirit further forms us as priests who serve him and one another with joy.

The Body of Christ

How often do I wander into church with low spirits and tired eyes! One such Sunday I looked up as the singing began. Across the room I saw my friend Jeremy. Though he was singing to God, he was doing so in a way that made it seem like he was also singing . . . at me. And probably at everyone else, too. It wasn't fake or forced. He simply sang in a way that invited others to join him:

> When Satan tempts me to despair
> And tells me of the guilt within
> Upward I look and see him there
> Who made an end to all my sin.[5]

---

[5] Charitie Lees Bancroft (1841–1923), "Before the Throne of God Above," 1863.

Amazingly, mysteriously, the Lord used Jeremy's facial expression to press the truth of that song into my heart. I started to sing along.

That brings us to our third portrait. A local church is the body of Christ. The lesson in this image is that in our worship, we should aim at mutual edification that results in unity.

In one sense, Christ's "body" is the universal church throughout space and time (e.g., Eph. 1:22–23). Yet there's another sense in which each local congregation em*bodies* Christ on earth. A church is made up of those who are united to Christ by faith and so are united to one another, with Christ as their head. As Paul tells the Corinthian church, "Now you [plural] are the body of Christ and individually members of it" (1 Cor. 12:27).

What do bodies do? They grow. They receive nourishment. They fight disease. Every member is an invaluable part of the whole (see 1 Corinthians 12). And every part helps "build up" every other part (Eph. 4:12).

That term "build up" occurs several times in 1 Corinthians 14, the most extended discussion in Scripture about what a church should do when it gathers:

- Verse 5: "The one who prophesies is greater than the one who speaks in tongues, unless someone interprets, so that the church may be *built up*."
- Verse 12: "So with yourselves, since you are eager for manifestations of the Spirit, strive to excel in *building up* the church."
- Verse 26: "What then, brothers? When you come together, each one has a hymn, a lesson, a revelation, a tongue, or an interpretation. Let all things be done for *building up*."

In sum, since a church is the body of Christ, edification should be at the center of a church's meeting.[6]

What does this mean for corporate worship?

- *We gather to edify and to be edified.* A "lone ranger" Christian is like a detached prosthetic limb. Our corporate worship should undermine self-centeredness. We come to be built up because we desperately need it—just as I needed Jeremy's encouragement that day. Yet also, in God's providence, other members need us to come and build them up too. We are simultaneously doctors and patients in God's hospital, binding up others' wounds and receiving the medicine our own souls need.

- *Corporate worship is discipleship.* God calls church members to minister to one another by speaking the truth in love (Eph. 4:12–15). We often imagine that taking place in small group Bible studies, one-on-one discipling relationships, and informal fellowship. And it does. But a church service is one of the primary settings in which believers speak the truth to one another. When we recite a creed, or read Scripture aloud together, or sing a Psalm, or vocalize "amen" after a prayer, we're not just following the service leader's directions. We are discipling one another and building up the body to maturity.

---

[6] The priority on edification in 1 Corinthians 12–14 also helps churches put debates about so-called "charismatic gifts" of the Holy Spirit (a misnomer, because all the Spirit's gifts are given according to his *charis,* his grace) into proper context. Whether a church concludes that gifts such as speaking in tongues, interpretation of tongues, prophecy, etc., should be expected today or not, the point is that all such gifts are meant to glorify Christ *by building up* the whole body. For an excellent defense of a "nuanced cessationism" position, which argues that certain gifts largely ceased with the completion of the New Testament canon, see Thomas Schreiner, *Spiritual Gifts: What They Are and Why They Matter* (Nashville: B&H, 2018). Though I hold to Schreiner's view, a strong argument for the continuation of such gifts today is presented by Andrew Wilson in *Spirit and Sacrament: An Invitation to Eucharismatic Worship* (Grand Rapids, MI: Zondervan, 2018).

- *Corporate worship should both reflect and contribute to a church's unity.* In 1 Corinthians 12, Paul teaches that every church member is essential. Not only has God given us each different gifts. He also intends for us to display his power through the supernatural unity we enjoy: "in one Spirit we were all baptized into one body—Jews or Greeks, slaves or free—and all were made to drink of one Spirit" (1 Cor. 12:13). This unity will make itself evident in a spirit of hospitality: those who have more power or privilege in this world will look for opportunities to serve and welcome those who have been oppressed or who are suffering. This unity will show up when members sing along gladly with songs that may not be in their favorite style, because they know the songs bring comfort to brothers or sisters who are older or younger than they are or who come from a different cultural background.

Since a church is the body of Christ, we worship as a unified whole. And our worship in turn further forms us into the mature, united people Christ calls us to be.

CONCLUSION

I'd much rather eat dinner with my family than alone. Our gathering at the table is one place where we showcase our distinct corporate identity. It's where we fellowship with one another. It's where we nourish and build one another up with the goal of greater unity.

As we've seen, it's the same with the local church. Our corporate worship is a feast. Christ himself hosts us at his banquet table. We gather in his honor to delight in the richest of fare. And he expects us to meet together, as one family. We are the outpost of his kingdom, the temple of his Spirit, the body he is nurturing toward maturity.

2

MUST WE GATHER?

Why does anyone go to church?

You've got lots of other options on Sunday morning. You could sleep in and enjoy a leisurely brunch. Catch up on your favorite TV shows. Take the kids to soccer practice.

And yet, tens of millions of people around the world keep getting out of bed—Sunday after Sunday after Sunday—to go to church.

Some do it out of duty. They assume it helps them get on God's good side. Others go to socialize, or to teach their children about morality. Some crave an emotional "high" to carry them through the week. Others seek intellectual stimulation or ethical instruction.

What about born-again believers? Hopefully you'd hear different answers: "I go to church to praise God," or "to learn about the Bible," or "to be encouraged through fellowship." But regardless of why we *think* we're going, there's a deeper theological reason behind it all: God gathers his people. If God has adopted you into his family, then *he* is the one who brings you to the family dinner table of corporate worship.

Think back to what we discussed in chapter 1. As a Christian, you're part of Christ's assembly, the church. You represent his kingdom. You're a Spirit-filled priest in his temple. You belong to his body. So when you walk into your church's gathering, God is working in you—and in everyone else—to get you there. He sovereignly draws his redeemed people together.

Christians *go* to church to worship because we *are* the church. Ecclesiology shapes doxology. To cultivate a richer understanding of corporate worship, we must recapture a sense of the wonder and gravity of the church's gathering.

In this chapter, we'll explore what it means for the church's worship that we are a gathered people. First, we need to consider how assembling together is an essential aspect of a church's life. Then, we'll turn to the deeper theological reality underlying the church's gathering: the fact that God initiates in love to bring his people together for his good purposes.

GATHERED TO BE A GATHERING

A local church is an assembly. If a church never meets, it is no church at all.

We easily take this truth for granted. The time of the worship meeting is often the first piece of information a church provides on its marquee or website. "Join us this Sunday at 10:30! All are welcome!"

Meeting, however, isn't just something churches *do*. A meeting is, in part, what a church *is*. God has saved us as individuals to *be* a corporate assembly.

We see this throughout Scripture. Picture the nation of Israel, rescued from Egypt and gathered together at Mount Sinai to hear God's law. Moses later referred to that seminal moment as "the day of *assembly*" (Deut. 9:10). At other key junctures in

Israel's history, the nation similarly gathered as an "assembly" before their covenant Lord (Judg. 20:2; 1 Kings 8:14; 1 Chron. 28:8).

The word in the Greek translation of the Old Testament for "assembly," *ekklesia*, is the same word the New Testament writers use to refer to the local church. It's simply the term for a gathering.[1] But when applied to the church, it carries the rich Old Testament connotations of standing together as God's chosen people.

So, what does the New Testament teach us about the local church assembly?

1. First, we see that churches gather regularly. Paul uses phrases like "when *you come together as a church*" and "*the whole church comes together*" (1 Cor. 11:18; 14:23).

2. Second, a church assembly is a distinct event. This is evident because Paul provides instructions on what believers should do "in church"—that is, in the church meeting. "*In church* I would rather speak five words with my mind in order to instruct others, than ten thousand words in a tongue" (1 Cor. 14:19); "if there is no one to interpret, let each of them keep silent *in church*" (v. 28).

3. Third, even large churches met as one body in the New Testament era. Thousands of believers belonged to the congregation at Jerusalem, yet they met "*all together* in Solomon's Portico" (Acts 5:12).

4. Fourth, the New Testament writers instruct churches to do activities that can only be done by meeting together: teaching and admonishing one another; singing psalms, hymns, and spiritual songs (Col. 3:16); reading

---

[1] See Acts 19:32 and 19:39, where *ekklesia* denotes non-Christian assemblies.

Scripture publicly (1 Tim. 4:13); and encouraging one another (Heb. 10:24–25). None of these can happen in a vacuum. And while it's true that many of these things can take place among smaller subsets of the church (such as your Tuesday night Bible study), we should assume that they belong first and foremost to the main congregational gathering, given the biblical emphasis on the whole church meeting together.[2]

5. Fifth, church discipline is an act of the gathered congregation. Jesus envisions "*the church*" as a whole, the *ekklesia*, speaking to the unrepentant sinner. In order to do this, they must be "*gathered*" in his name (Matt. 18:17, 20). Paul echoes this language as he instructs the Corinthians to implement church discipline "when you are *assembled* [same Greek word as *gathered* in Matt. 18:20] in the name of the Lord Jesus" (1 Cor. 5:4).

What's the picture? A church is a blood-bought people, devoted to the worship of the one true God. They're set apart from the world. They're committed to serving one another and loving their neighbors. And they do all this by *assembling* together in space and time.

A church is more than a gathering, of course. It gathers, then scatters, then gathers again. Its members continue to be part of the church throughout the week, as they serve and represent Christ in their homes, their workplaces, their neighborhoods. But a church is never *less* than a gathering.[3]

---

[2] Mark Dever, *The Church: The Gospel Made Visible* (Nashville: B&H Academic, 2012), 136.
[3] Here's how theologian Miroslav Volf puts it: "The life of the church is not exhausted in the act of assembly. Even if a church is not assembled, it does live on as the church in the mutual service its members render to one another and in its common mission to the world. . . . In its most concentrated form, however, the church does manifest itself concretely in the act of assembling for worship, and this is constitutive for its ecclesiality"

I used to live a few blocks from the United States Supreme Court. The nine justices who serve on my nation's highest judicial body are, in one sense, regular people like you and me. They walk the sidewalks and shop at local grocery stores. You might find yourself sitting next to one of them at a Washington Capitals hockey game or an opera at the Kennedy Center. They're all influential individuals on their own, of course, but in the deepest sense, *they are who they are* as an assembly.

When the Supreme Court justices meet *as a court* to make formal judgments, they take on a unique joint identity. Together, they wield an authority far greater than the sum of their parts. Thus, lawyers introduce their remarks not by saying, "May it please the justices," but instead, "May it please the Court"—singular. The Supreme Court is a corporate institution, one that normally depends on its nine members convening in space and time.

In a similar way, God has designed the local church as a people who meet. It doesn't work any other way.[4]

What makes the assembly such an important part of a church's identity?

First, the assembly makes the church visible *to itself*. Think of a big extended family that gathers for a photograph at the

---

(*After Our Likeness: The Church as the Image of the Trinity* [Grand Rapids, MI: Eerdmans, 1998], 137).

[4] W. B. Johnson, a nineteenth-century Baptist pastor, said it well: "A church is a congregation, a company of disciples, redeemed from sin and condemnation, associated together to perform certain duties, and to effect certain ends. *They are to meet every Lord's Day*, to engage in the duties of social worship, to combine their energies, and to act in concert as a band of soldiers under the Captain of their salvation" (*The Gospel Developed through the Government and Order of the Churches of Jesus Christ* [1846]. Reprinted in *Polity*, ed. Mark Dever [Washington: Nine Marks Ministries, 2001], 188, emphasis mine).

end of their annual reunion. They take the picture so they can *see* themselves and remember the bond they share.

Similarly, when a church gathers for corporate worship, the congregation is presented, as it were, to itself. Here's how theologian Everett Ferguson puts it: "In assembly, the church . . . becomes conscious of itself, confesses itself to be a distinct entity, shows itself to be what it is—a community (a people) gathered by the grace of God, dependent on him, and honoring him. The assembly allows the church to emerge in its true nature."[5]

This happens whenever a congregation meets. On Sundays at 10:30 a.m., my church, Capitol Hill Baptist, "emerges" in our century-old building on 6th Street. We meet all together— just one service, no separate campuses.[6]

Do you know what I see as this happens? I see Martina, whose husband recently passed away. She tears up while we sing "It Is Well with My Soul." I see Jared, the successful banker in the back row who is being discipled by Ben, an unemployed guy sitting in the balcony. I see John, a Jewish man who came to faith a few years ago while listening to a sermon here on the parable

---

[5] Everett Ferguson, *The Church of Christ: A Biblical Ecclesiology for Today* (Grand Rapids, MI: Eerdmans, 1996), 235.

[6] If you've been following my argument so far, you've probably already inferred that I believe that the biblical model for a local church is one that normally gathers as a single assembly. In other words, I would argue that a multisite or multiservice "church" is actually a collection of multiple, distinct churches. However, I hope that advocates of multisite and multiservice models can still appreciate many of the emphases on the church's gathering in this chapter. They will simply need to apply these points not to the church as a whole but to the various meetings consisting of portions of the church (as they conceive them). For a brief defense of the "one assembly" argument, see Dever, *The Church*, 132–136. For a book-length defense, see Jonathan Leeman, *One Assembly* (Wheaton, IL: Crossway, 2020). Arguments in favor of multisite churches appear in Brad House and Gregg Allison, *MultiChurch: Exploring the Future of Multisite* (Grand Rapids, MI: Zondervan, 2017); and J. D. Greear, "A Pastor Defends His Multisite Church" (February 25, 2010, https://www.9marks.org/article/pastor-defends-his-multi-site-church/).

of the Prodigal Son. His father opposes his trust in Christ, yet he gathers here with his new spiritual family every Lord's Day.

Are these folks ever at home due to illness, or away on vacation? Sure. But basically, I can expect to see them here every week. As I look across the gathering, I see believers who are helping one another follow Christ through persecution, cancer, miscarriage, addiction, depression, and more. And they've committed to doing that, in part, by assembling here *together*. They're singing the same songs, confessing the same faith in the same creed, hearing the same Scriptures read and the same sermon preached, sharing the same bread and the same cup.

Just as the sight of his bride makes a groom's heart swell with love, church members should overflow with affection for one another when they behold the assembly. *This is the people whom Jesus bought with his own blood. This is the people who have committed to care for me, put up with my faults, and point me to Christ again and again.*

Second, not only does assembling make the church visible to itself, it makes the church visible *to the universe*. Why did God join Jew and Gentile together into one body? He did this "so that through the church the manifold wisdom of God might now be made known to the rulers and authorities in the heavenly places" (Eph. 3:10).

Think about how this happens in a local church's assembly. A nineteen-year-old indie rock fan dressed in all black is singing "Great Is Thy Faithfulness," which our pianist accompanies in a decidedly non-indie style; he's harmonizing with the Colombian grandmother next to him. A man who's just been diagnosed with terminal cancer leads the congregation in a prayer of praise, and then his son-in-law is commissioned for the joyous task of church planting. At the end of the service, a Korean-American college student tells about how she recently placed her faith in Christ because several church members shared the gospel with her, and we all watch as she is baptized. When the gathering concludes, people hang around for forty-five minutes or longer, many of them discussing the sermon or praying together.

This sort of gathering, which by God's grace is a pretty normal Sunday for us, should leave the world speechless. Where else can you find such a bizarre mix of people, all praising the same triune God? Where else do folks who have very little else in common gather to bear each other's burdens? This bright witness for the gospel is possible because the church assembles.

The assembly is no less important in contexts that are more culturally homogenous. Even if everyone in the church looks alike (because everyone within fifty miles looks alike!) the congregation should still embody an otherworldly sort of love, commitment, and care for one another—one that they put on display by meeting together regularly.

I hope you're getting the picture. The better we understand the significance of the church's gathering, the sweeter and deeper our corporate worship will be. Consider how a robust view of the assembly protects us from some of the forces that tend to weaken our worship today:

- A strong theology of assembly combats *formalistic* worship. Since the gathering is a supernatural event in view of the watching cosmos (Eph. 3:10), it doesn't make sense to simply "go through the motions" out of a sense of duty or tradition as practiced by many nominal Christians.

- A strong theology of assembly combats *individualistic* worship. The service is a gathering of those who have committed to help one another endure to the end. This keeps us focused on the good of others, and it prevents us from seeing church as a "program" that's offered merely for our personal inspiration.
- A strong theology of assembly combats *consumer-oriented* worship. The good of the whole church is more important than being comfortable or having my preferences met. Each believer experiences the joyful freedom of taking the focus off self and putting it on God and others.

Finally, to put it positively, a strong theology of the assembly reminds us that God delights to pour out his presence among his people. There's a simple reason why meeting with God's people brings us such joy, according to the Puritan pastor David Clarkson—because God blesses his gathered people with his Spirit:

> The Lord engages himself to let forth as it were, a stream of his comfortable, quickening presence to every particular person that fears him, but when many of these particulars join together to worship God, then these several streams are united and meet in one. So that the presence of God, which, enjoyed in private, is but a stream, in public becomes a river, a river that makes glad the city of God.[7]

---

[7] David Clarkson, *The Works of David Clarkson, Vol. 3* (Carlisle, PA: Banner of Truth, 1988; originally published 1696), 190.

GATHERED BY GOD'S GRACIOUS INITIATIVE

The local church, then, *is* a gathering. But we don't assemble ourselves, on our own initiative, in our own strength. We become a gathering only because God draws us together. He is the one who makes us a body, and he is the one who brings the body together each Lord's Day.

We gather by God's grace.

When we recognize God's initiative in gathering his people, it reframes how we conceive of corporate worship. Here's what I mean: It's common to hear people describe worship as "our response to God." While that captures a key truth, it isn't the whole picture. Before we respond to God, God first works in us.

Think of Romans 12:1, one of the most famous verses on worship in the New Testament. It's about serving God with our whole lives, not just on Sundays. But it illustrates this important point: Paul says, "Present your bodies as a living sacrifice, holy and acceptable to God, which is your spiritual worship." That's what *we're* called to do, Sunday through Saturday, every moment. We offer ourselves entirely to God's glory.

But how can sinners like us do this? Only because of God's mercy and sovereignty. We must not forget that Paul makes this appeal "by the mercies of God" (Rom. 12:1). We can offer ourselves to God only because Christ first offered himself for us. Then, having saved us, God sovereignly grants in us that which he asks of us. In the verse immediately preceding this one, Paul explains, "From him and through him and to him are all things. To him be glory forever" (Rom. 11:36). *To him are all things*, yes. But all things are also *from* and *through* him. That includes the bodies and lives that we offer back to him. It includes our worship, both individually and corporately. So, when we worship God, it is *God himself* who is working in us, "both to will and to work for his good pleasure" (Phil. 2:13).

Let's think about how this truth should inform our corporate gatherings. God takes the initiative when the church meets. To put it as strongly as possible, worship is *God's work* first, before it is ours. God the Father grants us to honor him in and through our mediator, God the Son, by the power of God the Spirit. Our worship originates in the triune God and resounds to the eternal glory of the triune God.

Picture a family with young kids exchanging presents on Christmas morning. Five-year-old Jonathan and three-year-old Hannah don't have any money of their own. Yet they can't wait to give a beautiful gold necklace to Mommy and a shiny new tool kit to Daddy. How did they pay for these gifts? Their parents bought them, of course. But that doesn't make Jonathan and Hannah any less sincere in giving them. And it doesn't make the parents any less glad to receive them.

In the same way, corporate worship is a gift we receive and give back to God, the Giver of all things. As the theologians put it, the triune God is *both* the chief "Subject" and the chief "Object" of our worship.[8]

It's common to speak of what a church does on Sunday mornings as a "worship service." That's true, but we must put

---

[8] E.g., Marva Dawn, *A Royal "Waste" of Time: The Splendor of Worshiping God and Being Church for the World* (Grand Rapids, MI: Eerdmans, 1999), 152–153.

55

the accent where it belongs: God serves us before we serve him. *He* ministers to us. *He* blesses us. *He* reveals himself to us. *He* pours out grace upon undeserved grace. Only once he serves us do we serve him. And even then, we serve him with the strength that he alone provides.

Consider how God makes it possible for us to worship him in the first place.

God the Father foreknows and predestines a people for himself on the basis of his own loving will (Rom. 8:29; Eph. 1:4–5; 1 Pet. 1:1–2).[9] He calls sinners to trust him, he justifies the guilty, and he transforms us from idolaters into worshipers (Rom. 8:30; 1 Cor. 6:11; Eph. 2:5; 1 Thess. 1:9).

God the Son is the perfect Worshiper. He lives a life fully pleasing to the Father. He then offers himself as a sacrifice in our place, mediates a new covenant to us, and even now intercedes for us (Matt. 26:28; Heb. 7:25; 9:15; 10:12), opening the way for us to draw near to God (Heb. 10:22).

God the Spirit illumines our hearts to know the Father through the Son, enables us to call on Jesus as Lord, regenerates us from death to life, and prays for us (John 3:6–8; 1 Cor. 2:10–12; 12:3; Rom. 8:26–27).

But not only does God enable our worship in the first place, he ministers to us each time we gather:

- God manifests his presence in our midst: "there am I among them" (Matt. 18:20); "he will . . . declare that God is really among you" (1 Cor. 14:25).

---

[9] C. E. B. Cranfield, "Divine and Human Action: The Biblical Concept of Worship," *Interpretation* 12 (1958): 390–391. I am indebted to Cranfield throughout this section.

- God reveals himself to us, instructs us, and comforts us through his Word read, sung, and preached (Col. 3:16; 2 Tim. 3:16–17; 4:2; Heb. 4:12; 2 Pet. 1:21).
- God grants us "participation" in the body and blood of Christ at the Lord's Supper (1 Cor. 10:16–17).
- God convicts and converts unbelievers through the church's teaching (1 Cor. 14:24–25). As with Ezekiel's vision of dead bones coming to life at the preaching of God's Word (Ezekiel 37), God grants faith "from hearing the word of Christ" (Rom. 10:17).
- God builds up the body as believers use their Spirit-given gifts to strengthen one another (Eph. 4:11–16; 1 Cor. 12:7; 14:26).

Bryan Chapell summarizes it well: "God is not only the chief audience of our worship; by his Word and Spirit, he is also the true speaker, singer, and prayer."[10]

Here are several reasons why this matters:

1. First, a proper focus on God's initiative highlights the Trinitarian dimensions of corporate worship. God the Father assembles those who are united to Christ together in the presence of his Holy Spirit. Through the Spirit's indwelling, we fellowship together with the Father in Christ our mediator by hearing his Word and partaking of his Supper.

2. Second, appreciating God's initiative helps safeguard us from a man-centered, works-righteousness approach in worship. According to theologian Nicholas Wolterstorff, one of the chief problems with the medieval Roman

---

[10] Bryan Chapell, *Christ-Centered Worship: Letting the Gospel Shape Our Practice* (Grand Rapids, MI: Baker Academic, 2009), 119.

Catholic mass was that God's action was "lost from view. The actions were all human." In returning to a biblical focus on God's gracious initiative, the Protestant Reformers recaptured an understanding of the gathering as "God's action and our faithful reception of that action."[11]

3. Third, when we see our corporate worship as originating from God, it attunes us to God's purposes for the church as a whole body. In 1 Corinthians 12:4–11, we learn that God gives believers various gifts to exercise when the church meets, but these "manifestation[s] of the Spirit" all have the same goal: "the common good" of the church (12:7). When God "empowers" us for corporate worship, he binds us to one another in unity (12:11).

4. Fourth, the fact that God is in charge of the worship gathering teaches us to treasure our fellow church members. It is not random happenstance that your congregation has its own unique mix of people: "God arranged the members in the body, each one of them, as he chose" (1 Cor. 12:18). God's sovereign will is for me to gather with the specific believers at *my* local church—warts, disagreements, awkwardness, and all. Since that's the case, I'd better stop complaining about their faults and get to work loving them. After all, that's what they've done for me.

5. Fifth, since God calls the meeting, what we do when we meet is his prerogative. Hughes Oliphant Old puts it this way: "The worship of the church is a matter of divine activity rather than human creativity."[12] Far from restrictive or stifling, this truth actually frees us from

---

[11] Nicholas Wolterstorff, "The Reformed Liturgy," in *Major Themes in the Reformed Tradition,* ed. Donald K. McKim (Eugene, OR: Wipf & Stock, 1998), 287, 290.
[12] Hughes Oliphant Old, "John Calvin and the Prophetic Criticism of Worship," in *John Calvin and the Church: A Prism of Reform,* ed. Timothy George (Louisville: Westminster John Knox, 1990), 234.

the shackles of human innovation in worship. I'll discuss this idea, often called the "regulative principle" of corporate worship, more in a later chapter.

6. Sixth, and finally, the primacy of God's initiative means we should gather to receive his blessing. While it is true that worship involves God-oriented sacrifice and obedience, it begins with "a hearing and a receiving."[13] We gather as needy, hungry children, in utter dependence on our all-sufficient Father. As we meet, God comforts. He convicts. He equips. He nourishes. He sanctifies. He speaks. He sustains. As Sunday looms and your week comes to an end, have you ever thirsted for the replenishing waters of God's goodness in the corporate worship service? That's the way it's supposed to be. God assembles us to give us what we most need: Christ his Son.

What a joy and privilege to meet with God's people, gathered by his grace. Now that we've considered this foundational reality, we're ready to discuss what God intends to do among his gathered people when we meet. What are the purposes for the worship gathering? That's what we'll explore in our next chapter.

---

[13] Cranfield, "Divine and Human Action," 392.

3

WHY DOES GOD GATHER US?

God is sovereign. The worship service is his idea. He gathers us together and then he takes the lead in serving us, making it possible for us to serve him.

So why does God gather us? What are his purposes and priorities for the assembled church? What does he call us to do when we meet?

Here's my answer: *God gathers us (1) unto his glory, (2) for our mutual good, (3) before the world's gaze.*

GOD GATHERS US UNTO HIS GLORY: EXALTATION

You can hear the thunderous roar of Niagara Falls as far as twenty miles away. At its peak, 2,382 metric tons of water cascade down the 188-foot cliff every second.

It's staggering to comprehend such majesty. Yet, although the falls seem forbidding, many visitors feel compelled to get closer. They board the *Maid of the Mist* ship to hear the thunder of water on rock and to get soaked by the spray.

The church gathers to hear and behold the glorious One, the One who stands above the entire universe. He is the Creator, the Designer of Niagara Falls and countless other wonders. Filled with reverent fear, we approach God to adore his unrivaled beauty.

God gathers us to glorify him.

Praise is the natural response of redeemed creatures. Early Christians praised God as they met in the temple (Acts 2:47). We no longer offer the animal sacrifices required by the old covenant but rather a "sacrifice of praise" (Heb. 13:15). We "do all to the glory of God" (1 Cor. 10:31), both during church and the rest of the week. As we sing, we make "melody to the Lord" (Eph. 5:19).

D. A. Carson puts it well: worship involves "ascribing all honor and worth to [our] Creator-God precisely because he is worthy, delightfully so."[1]

And we do so *together*, as an assembled church. Cue the Psalms: "Shout for joy, *all* you upright in heart!" (Ps. 32:11). "Oh, magnify the LORD with me, and let us exalt his name *together!*" (34:3). "Sing aloud to God *our* strength" (81:1). "Let *us* make a joyful noise to him with songs of praise!" (95:2). "Let *the redeemed of the LORD* say so" (107:2). We could go on and on. The point is clear: exaltation is the heartbeat of God's gathered people.

What ought to characterize a corporate service focused on exalting God?

First, *gravity*.[2] "Let us offer to God acceptable worship, with reverence and awe, for our God is a consuming fire"

---

[1] D. A. Carson, "Worship under the Word," in *Worship By the Book*, ed. D. A. Carson (Grand Rapids, MI: Zondervan, 2002), 26.
[2] John Piper has popularized the helpful catchphrase "gravity and gladness" as a description of biblical worship. See his *Gravity and Gladness: The Pursuit of God in Corporate Worship* (Wheaton, IL: Crossway, 2010).

(Heb. 12:28–29). A God-centered service should not indulge our appetites for saccharine spirituality. Approaching the living God is like gazing in awe at the height of Mount Everest, not wandering into a video arcade. We should sing songs that beckon our hearts to delight in God's attributes and deeds. Pastors should lead substantive prayers of praise and confession, since God is honored when we adore him directly in prayer, as well as when we mourn our sins and plead for his mercy (1 John 1:7–9).

Second, *gladness*. "Rejoice always," Paul instructed the assembly in Thessalonica (1 Thess. 5:16, 27). Our services should reflect the life-altering reality that Christ is risen. When prodigal sons and daughters meet at the Father's banquet table of corporate worship, it is "fitting to celebrate and be glad" (Luke 15:32).

Third, *gratitude*. Bob Kauflin writes, "Magnifying God's greatness *begins* with the proclamation of objective, biblical truths about God, but it *ends* with the expression of deep and holy affections toward God."[3] Since we can approach God only through the redemptive work of Christ, the rich aroma of thanksgiving should flavor our worship (Eph. 5:20).

Of course, the right combination of gravity, gladness, and gratitude will look different in different cultures. Yet these marks should all show up on Sundays. Some churches excel in demonstrating gravity, but a concern about becoming "over-emotional" keeps them from much feeling at all. Other churches excel in practicing gladness and gratitude. The music

---

[3] Bob Kauflin, *Worship Matters: Leading Others to Encounter the Greatness of God* (Wheaton, IL: Crossway, 2008), 65.

starts and enthusiasm flows fast. But the service lacks depth and seriousness. It feels more like youth group for grown-ups.

With that in mind, consider the connection between the health of a church and its ability to exalt God's glory. A church infested with gossip and division will have a tough time setting its focus on God's truthfulness on Sunday mornings. A church with negligent or heavy-handed leadership will struggle to submit to God's good authority. A church that tolerates serious, outward, unrepented sin is in danger of ignoring God's holiness rather than delighting in it (see 1 Corinthians 5).[4] The opposite of all these is true as well. Churches that challenge unholiness through discipleship and discipline say something about God's holy love. In short, the healthier a church, the more God-centered its worship will be.

The connection between health and God's glory goes in the other direction, too. Corporate worship should mold a congregation into a people more and more ravished by the beauty of God. Each Sunday meeting reorients a congregation's spiritual compass. We gather, and God sets our wayward course back to where it needs to be: toward himself.

To put it another way, we become like what we worship. If we serve idols, we'll end up like them: powerless, purposeless, and worthless (Ps. 115:8). But as a congregation beholds the true God through corporate worship character-

---

[4] This is why many historic churches included corrective church discipline in the Sunday service, usually as part of preparation for the Lord's Supper. A church that practices loving, biblical discipline is precisely the sort of congregation that can expect to enjoy God-centered worship. See Jonathan Gibson and Mark Earngey, "Worshiping in the Tradition: Principles from the Past for the Present," in *Reformation Worship: Liturgies from the Past for the Present* (Greensboro, NC: New Growth, 2018), 59–61.

ized by gravity, gladness, and gratitude, it will become more
and more like him.

GOD GATHERS US FOR OUR MUTUAL GOOD: EDIFICATION

Exaltation is the vertical dimension of our corporate response
to God's initiating grace. Edification is the horizontal dimension. Both take place at the same time. As we exalt God, we
edify one another.

Hundreds of the great hymns of the faith give us words to
praise God and encourage the body of Christ at the same time.
"A mighty fortress is *our* God." "How deep the Father's love for
us." "What a friend *we* have in Jesus."

These songs reflect the biblical teaching that those who
are filled with the Spirit show it by "addressing *one another*"
when we make melody to the Lord (Eph. 5:19). Our unity and
our praise are connected: "May the God of endurance and encouragement grant you to live in such harmony with one another [edification], in accord with Christ Jesus, that together
you may with one voice glorify the God and Father of our Lord
Jesus Christ [exaltation]" (Rom. 15:5–6).

When you think about it, we're familiar with the idea of
addressing multiple audiences at once. At bedtime, when the
whole family is around, I might say something like this to my
wife, while winking at our daughter: "*Someone* did a great job
of obeying my instructions while we were at the park today!"
I inform my wife, but my daughter knows that I want her to
receive encouragement from my report.

Corporate worship is similar. While we address our worship to God, we simultaneously spur one another on: *Listen*

to these praises! Delight your soul in the Lord! Take comfort in his promises!

This is one reason why Paul insists that everything said or sung in a church service should be intelligible to everyone there (1 Cor. 14:2–5). The whole church should benefit spiritually from every word, every song, every prayer.

This is also why Paul tells the church at Corinth to use their gifts to build up the whole body. Some in that congregation, it seems, craved the "flashy" gifts of the Spirit. Paul corrects them. The gifts you use in corporate worship *aren't* mainly for you, he teaches in 1 Corinthians 14. They're for everyone.

Here's how Paul says the same thing one chapter earlier: "the greatest of these is love" (1 Cor 13:13). Should you take the Lord's Supper before the whole body has gathered (11:21)? No, because love is patient (13:4). Should you look down on those with seemingly less important gifts (12:21–25)? No, because love does not envy or boast (13:4). Should you ignore those who are suffering (12:26)? No, because love bears all things, hopes all things (13:7). Should you take pride in speaking in tongues (14:2)? No, because tongues will cease, but love never ends (13:8).

We gather to love one another as Christ has loved us. This truth revolutionizes our approach to the Sunday service:

- Songs of praise to God are also tools for teaching each other God's Word (Col. 3:16–17). When you become a church member, you also become a Sunday school teacher— by opening your mouth in congregational singing.
- We attend church to receive from God (see chapter 2), but *also* to pour out service to others. Church members

should arrive in prayerful expectation that God intends to use them to bless someone else in need.

- We don't just think about our own lives during corporate prayer, but we apply the prayers to brothers and sisters whom we love. As the pastor prays that we'd share the gospel with others, I pray that would be especially true of Emily, who recently told me about a non-Christian co-worker she has been hoping to talk with about Jesus. As he prays that families and single members would build thriving relationships together, I pray that would happen between Tony and the Smiths.

- Everyone has a job to do. A church where folks sit back and passively absorb whatever's happening "up front" is a church that subtly undermines the priority of mutual edification. For sure, the elders whom God has called to lead his flock should take the initiative to prepare the meal. But we all get to serve it to one another—even if our part is as seemingly insignificant as joining in a corporate reading of Scripture, singing along to the hymns, and passing the bread and the cup to the person next to us.

- There's no room for anonymity when the church meets. David Peterson, meditating on 1 Corinthians 14, argues that it is inappropriate to design our gatherings "primarily to facilitate private communion with God."[5] Very practically, therefore, I appreciate being part of a church where the lights stay on. I also like how our seats are arranged in a semi-circle. We can see one another's faces and hear one another's voices. The Bible doesn't require these practical and architectural decisions, of course. But these details say something loud and clear: "This is a church where we minister to one another."

---

[5] David Peterson, *Engaging with God: A Biblical Theology of Worship* (Downers Grove, IL: IVP Academic, 1992), 214.

Exaltation and edification are mutually reinforcing. We can't separate them. Glorifying God encourages others, and loving our brothers and sisters brings delight to God. The vertical and horizontal belong together, every Sunday.

GOD GATHERS US BEFORE THE WORLD'S GAZE: EVANGELISM

As we glorify God and do one another good during the church's meeting, God also intends for our worship to take place before the world's gaze. In other words, our gatherings should be evangelistic.

In the Old Testament, the praise of God's people was a public witness before the pagan peoples surrounding Israel. "I will praise you, O LORD, among the nations" (Ps. 18:49). "Declare his glory among the nations, his marvelous works among all the peoples!" (Ps. 96:3). "May God be gracious to us and bless us and make his face to shine upon us, that your way be known on earth, your saving power among all nations" (Ps. 67:1–2).

As we've already seen, the New Testament envisions unbelievers attending Christian meetings, hearing the good news of Jesus, and being converted. Paul writes, "But if all prophesy, and an unbeliever or outsider enters, he is convicted by all, he is called to account by all, the secrets of his heart are disclosed, and so, falling on his face, he will worship God and declare that God is really among you" (1 Cor. 14:24–25).

We assemble, then, with the expectation that God delights to give new life to the lost who attend our services through the proclamation of the gospel of Jesus Christ. So far, so good, right?

Not so fast. In our day and age, we need to think carefully about how evangelism fits in our services. Over the last several decades, a popular philosophy of ministry has urged churches to reimagine the church gathering with the unbeliever in mind. Although it is a broad movement, churches in this stream have generally prioritized attracting unchurched "seekers" by designing worship services that are uplifting, casual, and focused on life issues of interest to non-Christians.[6]

I served on staff at such a church many years ago. That congregation loves Jesus and the lost. It's full of great folks with good intentions. Yet, during my time there, I planned and led worship services that illustrated this trend. When picking songs, we looked for music that we thought unbelievers would enjoy. When planning sermons, we gravitated toward topical series on matters that we presumed our neighbors cared about, rather than preaching through books of Scripture. We avoided rough theological edges. We spent a lot of time preparing graphics, PowerPoint slides, video clips, and announcement skits, all to make the services feel less "churchy" and more accessible to newcomers. We explicitly told believers that the Sunday service was mainly a venue for introducing friends and neighbors to Christianity, while the place to grow deeper in their own faith was a midweek small group Bible study.

Now, after years of reflection, I think that approach was misguided. Of course, there are important lessons we can learn from

---

[6] Ed Dobson, an early proponent of this approach, identified the following six characteristics of such a service: "Informal; Contemporary (nontraditional); No pressure for involvement or commitment; Relevant to these people's needs; Casual, 'laid-back' format; Visually appealing" (*Starting a Seeker Sensitive Service: How Traditional Churches Can Reach the Unreached* [Grand Rapids, MI: Zondervan, 1993], 27). Interestingly, Dobson was proposing an evangelistic meeting that would take place on Saturday nights. The service outlined in his book wasn't a replacement for the Sunday morning church gathering. Nevertheless, over the ensuing years these six characteristics increasingly typified Sunday worship services at many churches across America.

that church and others like it. They teach us to care for the lost and to remove unnecessary barriers that might keep unbelievers from hearing the good news. However, by and large, the drive to be "sensitive" to seekers has tended to result in church services that are in fact oriented *first and foremost* toward unbelievers but are deficient in the nourishment that the congregation needs.[7]

I fear that this trend in evangelicalism has subtly trained a generation of pastors and worship leaders to make evangelism what we might call the "organizing principle" of a church meeting. The result is that for many who plan services, it's easy to fall into a default posture of structuring the gathering with an eye toward the unbeliever first.

I agree that our services should be evangelistic. But, paradoxically, the way God calls us to be evangelistic when we meet is *not* to consider the non-Christian visitor our primary audience. Rather, the service is a family meeting of God's people, gathered around his throne for the priorities of exaltation and edification that we discussed earlier. But, in God's surprising grace, this is precisely the way he intends to use our worship services to draw people to Christ.

To see this, let's take a closer look at 1 Corinthians 14:24–25. Paul's point in this chapter is to convince the Corinthians

---

[7] Swee Hong Lim and Lester Ruth explain the viewpoint that led to this outcome. Their analysis is worth quoting in full: "Church growth thinking reawakened a liturgical pragmatism that has characterized much of American Protestantism since the branding and promoting of camp meetings in the Second Great Awakening at the beginning of the nineteenth century. The mind frame is thoroughly American because of its democratic and capitalistic assumptions about numerical validation. Those assumptions create a liturgical pragmatism driven by numbers: What works to produce the greatest numbers in worship? When fused with evangelistic concerns, the perspective creates an approach to worship that assesses worship from the outside in: What works best in worship for the people who are not here and are not members already?" (*Lovin' on Jesus: A Concise History of Contemporary Worship* [Nashville: Abingdon, 2017], 21).

that prophecy is more edifying than speaking in tongues because all can understand it. He wants the whole church to be built up. He also envisions an "unbeliever or outsider" entering the meeting (14:24). What this person hears—it might be better to say *overhears*—in the meeting is the wonderful sound of Christians prophesying in order to build one another up. The outsider listens in, understands, falls on his face, trusts in Christ, and joins in the worship of God.

Exaltation and edification are not at odds with evangelism. They're exactly what the Lord uses to convert unbelievers in our midst.

How? Let's get practical. What does a worship service that is focused on glorifying God and doing good to the saints, *and is therefore* a powerful evangelistic witness, actually look like?

First, such a service is filled with the gospel. After all, heralding the wondrous news of Jesus Christ both brings praise to God and encourages the church. We glorify God's character when we announce that he is a holy Creator and Judge to whom all humankind is accountable. We exalt his righteousness when we declare that all people have sinned, fallen short of his glory, and deserve his just wrath. We magnify the infinite wonders of his grace when we proclaim that God's Son, Jesus Christ, was born of a virgin, lived a perfect life, offered himself as a sacrifice for sinners, rose from the grave, ascended to heaven, was seated at the Father's right hand, and will return in victory over sin and death to usher in a new heaven and new earth. We praise his mercy and power when we announce that, by his Spirit, God grants gifts of repentance and faith so that the guilty might be justified, the filthy washed clean, and the dead made alive in Christ. Hallelujah, God be praised!

Such astounding truths warm believers' hearts. We never graduate from the gospel. We need to hear it again and again. A gospel-saturated service is precisely how we edify God's people. So it's no wonder that an outsider should hear the good news of Jesus if he or she attends.

Let me get even more particular, though. Not only should our services overflow with the gospel, they should preserve its hard edges. Try conducting a "gospel audit" of your services by examining your church's songs, prayers, Scripture readings, and sermons, particularly with an eye toward those aspects of the good news that are most provocative. Do they regularly mention sin, judgment, and God's wrath against wickedness? Do they teach that Jesus is Lord as well as Savior? Do they call believers to a life of repentance and bearing one's cross? I'm not saying that every single prayer or hymn needs to have a *compact and complete* gospel summary, like the one I provided a few paragraphs ago. That would get laborious and repetitive. I simply mean that the news of what God has done for us in Christ—even and especially the parts that are most offensive to our sinful flesh—should be easy to find, all throughout the service. Don't save the gospel for a two-minute, tacked-on "presentation" at the end of the sermon.

Second, in planning such a service, we should pray for God to reveal himself and grant new life to the spiritually dead. In our sinful and depraved state, no unbeliever truly "seeks" God. As the psalmist says,

The LORD looks down from heaven on the children of man,
>to see if there are any who understand,
>who seek after God.

They have all turned aside; together they have become corrupt;
>there is none who does good,
>not even one. (Ps. 14:2–3)

That means, theologically speaking, there is only one "seeker" present at your church services. Jesus taught that *God* is the one "seeking" a people who worship in spirit and truth (John 4:23).

This reality should lead us to declare the gospel simply, in reliance on God's strength, without gimmicks or artificial adornment. We must herald Christ crucified in our gatherings (Rom. 10:14–17), but God is the one who gives faith (John 6:44; Eph. 2:8–9).

Third, the entire service should stand as a testimony of our countercultural hope. Mike Cosper expresses this with a wonderful phrase, "worship as protest."[8] In our corporate services, he says, we testify to a kingdom that cannot be shaken, a beacon of truth in the darkness, a Deliverer infinitely more powerful than the false saviors of politics, power, sex, money, and success. When we focus our gathering on exaltation and edification, we hold out the water of life to a thirsty world and call it to turn away from those broken cisterns that never satisfy. This is the real "worship war": a battle against idolatry, calling all people to serve the true King.[9]

---

[8] Mike Cosper, *Rhythms of Grace: How the Church's Worship Tells the Story of the Gospel* (Wheaton, IL: Crossway, 2013), 101–102.

[9] Gibson and Earngey, "Worshiping in the Tradition," 49.

Fourth, even as we prioritize exaltation and edification, we should aim to make our services intelligible for unbelievers. That's Paul's point in 1 Corinthians 14: when we build one another up, we should do it in a language that believers as well as unbelievers understand. Bryan Chapell's approach is the right one: "We do not focus on seekers. We do not forget them, either."[10] Use a Bible translation that unchurched folks can understand. Clarify what's going on throughout the service: Why are we singing right now? Why are we praying? Putting money in a basket? Dunking people under water? Use rich biblical and theological terms, but explain them for the sake of unbelievers and new believers alike.

In just about every sermon, my pastor, Mark, will speak directly to non-Christian visitors, usually with a provocative, open-ended question related to his sermon text. This practice shows unbelievers that you know they are here and that you're trying to understand their concerns. It also helps model for the congregation how to talk to non-Christian friends.

God intends our corporate worship to provoke the watching world. Our gatherings not only proclaim the gospel. They also display a gospel people, a foretaste of the coming new creation.

So we conclude these first three chapters where they began: with the church. God has made us his people. We are the outpost of his kingdom, the temple of his Spirit, the body of Christ. He gathers us by his grace. And when we meet, God works powerfully among us to bring about his own exaltation

---

[10] Bryan Chapell, *Christ-Centered Worship: Letting the Gospel Shape Our Practice* (Grand Rapids, MI: Baker Academic, 2009), 139.

and our edification. As he does, he works in and through us as a local church to proclaim the gospel to the lost. And by his grace, he brings new believers into the church. They then join us in giving glory to God and doing good to the saints. What wisdom God has shown!

Having set the stage for how a rich understanding of the local church should transform our approach to the gathering, we are now ready to take a closer look at the content and shape of a worship service.

4

WHAT SHOULD WE DO WHEN WE GATHER?

The Major League Baseball umpire's manual has 158 pages. It's full of regulations that govern the game. Sadly, this book has no power to turn my beloved New York Mets into a winning team! But it ensures that players truly play *baseball*, not some other game.

Is it overly strict to have such a long rulebook? Is it too severe? I think most athletes and fans would argue the opposite: baseball is a beautiful game *because* it's a regulated game. Anyone who followed the Houston Astros' 2017–2018 cheating scandal would say so. The same is true of all other sports: It's not drudgery to play according to the book. You're upholding the game's design. When you play, you focus not on the manual but on the joy of the game.

In this chapter, I'll argue that corporate worship is likewise a "regulated" activity. Having seen what a church is and why God gathers local churches each week, we now turn to consider the question, *what specific activities can and should a church do when it gathers for corporate worship?* After all, Scripture commands believers to gather regularly (Heb. 10:24–25). Pastors must decide, Sunday after Sunday, what their church members will *do* when they meet on the Lord's Day.

Here's the main point for this chapter: *God, by his Word, governs what the local church should do when it gathers.* I want to persuade you to adopt what has been called the "regulative principle" of corporate worship. This is the idea that God hasn't left it up to us to decide what acts of gathered worship are valid. He has revealed his will to us in his Word. We worship according to his design and intent.

Churches that follow this principle won't all look identical. The specific ways they put it into practice will vary across eras and cultures. But all congregations that embrace the regulative principle affirm the basic notion that God defines for us, in his Word, how we should engage with him in corporate worship.

Here's how the Protestant Reformer John Hooper put it in 1550: "Nothing should be used in the Church which has not either the express Word of God to support it, or otherwise is a thing indifferent in itself."[1] By "indifferent," he means something that doesn't pertain to the essence of our worship, such as the time when we meet or the color of the chairs. The "express Word of God" includes both explicit commands and implicit examples in Scripture.

This makes sense when we reflect on the nature of corporate worship. Recall that God is the one who gathers the

---

[1] John Hooper, "The Regulative Principle and Things Indifferent," in *The Reformation of the Church: A Collection of Reformed and Puritan Documents on Church Issues*, ed. Iain Murray (Edinburgh: Banner of Truth Trust, 1965), 55.

church and works in our midst. Our worship is generated by his gracious initiative. He is the central actor. That means *he* decides what happens when the church meets. The service is his prerogative, not ours.

Recall too that the church's meeting is a corporate phenomenon, through and through. A church service is not a bunch of individual Christians who happen to be standing next to one another, offering their own worship to God through a private portal of praise. It's a family gathering. That means when we plan a service, we must ask ourselves if we have warrant to require the whole church to engage in each act of worship.

THE REGULATIVE PRINCIPLE IS A POSTURE

Scripture tells us *what* we should do in the public worship of God, but it doesn't dictate every last detail about *how* to do it. Sometimes people protest that the regulative principle cannot be valid because the Bible doesn't tell us if we should meet at 10 a.m. or 11 a.m., stand or sit, or sing in the key of C or D. But those sorts of objections misunderstand what the regulative principle is about.

The regulative principle is a posture regarding the essential acts or "elements" of corporate worship. It's a way of saying that when we consider the main strokes of what to do when the church gathers, our basic instinct should be to lead the gathered church to do only what Scripture commands.

How do we arrive at this posture? Let's consider three main arguments.[2]

---

[2] For more, see J. Ligon Duncan III, "Does God Care How We Worship?" and "Foundations for Biblically Directed Worship," in *Give Praise to God: A Vision for Reforming Worship*, ed.

First, an argument from idolatry. Consider Exodus 32:5, where we hear the tragic story of the golden calf. "When Aaron saw [the calf], he built an altar before it. And Aaron made a proclamation and said, 'Tomorrow shall be a feast to the LORD.'" Whoa—did you catch that? The people intended to worship the LORD—Yahweh—by presenting a feast to a statue! God rightly condemned this, and in doing so he made it clear that the second commandment isn't merely a restriction on worshiping the wrong gods. It also forbids worshiping the true God in the wrong way.

The golden calf incident shows that sincerity is not enough to make our worship acceptable. We can have sincere intentions—"authenticity," to use a current buzzword—and yet fatally misstep. Romans 1:22 reminds us that though idolatry is pure folly, it always seems wise to those who engage in it. Calvin said that the human heart is a perpetual idol factory. He wasn't just talking about worshiping other gods. He meant that we are continually tempted to approach the true God in idolatrous ways, ways that subtly refashion him according to our own thoughts and desires.

The only safe way to worship God is according to his revealed will. The regulative principle protects us from spoiling our corporate worship with idolatrous human ideas. After all, we're talking about a God who is a "consuming fire" (Heb. 12:29). God condemned Nadab and Abihu not because their worship was insincere, but because it was "unauthorized." They did something "which he had not commanded them" (Lev. 10:1).

Philip Graham Ryken, Derek W. H. Thomas, and J. Ligon Duncan III (Phillipsburg, NJ: P&R, 2003), 17–73.

Second, an argument from the doctrine of God. Jesus taught the woman at the well, "God is spirit, and those who worship him must worship in spirit and truth" (John 4:24). Our worship must be consistent with God's true nature, and it must correspond to the truth that he has revealed. In this passage, Jesus corrects the Samaritan woman's ideas about the proper place of worship. She thinks worship should be on a particular mountain. Jesus tells her she's wrong: we worship in and through the Spirit. The takeaway? There's a right and a wrong *way* to worship.

Since God is transcendent and incomprehensible, why would we trust our own invented ideas for how to praise him when gathered with his people? Even Adam and Eve, before they fell into sin, needed God's instruction for how to engage with him (see Gen. 2:16–17). All we know about God we know because he has revealed it to us. We shouldn't assume that we can figure out how to worship such a God on our own.

Third, an argument from the sufficiency of Scripture. Consider 2 Timothy 3:16–17: "All Scripture is breathed out by God and profitable for teaching, for reproof, for correction, and for training in righteousness, that the man of God may be complete, equipped for *every good work*." Corporate worship is one of the foremost good works to which God calls us. Since Scripture equips us for *every* good work, then we need not step outside God's Word to find out how to worship.

ELEMENTS, FORMS, AND CIRCUMSTANCES

In conversations about the regulative principle of worship, many theologians distinguish between three key terms:

elements, forms, and circumstances. *Elements* of worship are the activities that Scripture positively calls us to perform in our corporate devotion to God. The regulative principle is primarily concerned with determining which elements of worship are biblical. Following our Protestant Reformation heritage, we can summarize these elements under five headings: read the Word, pray the Word, preach the Word, sing the Word, and see the Word (summarized and depicted in baptism and the Lord's Supper).[3]

Forms of worship refer to the manner in which we go about the elements of worship. If you're furnishing a kitchen, you need certain basic elements, like a stove. But what form of stove? Electric? Gas? Toaster oven? It depends on your time and place. Should we read corporately or responsively? Should we sing in a major or minor key? Should we pray extemporaneously or prepare our prayers in advance? These, I would argue, are questions of form, questions that the regulative principle does not strictly address. To answer the questions of form, we need wisdom. Different churches may come to different judgments. That doesn't mean these questions are unimportant. Certain forms may be more or less wise. The Bible may not specify exactly which forms to use, but it gives us principles and wisdom that guide us as we seek those forms which tend most to exaltation, edification, and evangelism.

---

[3] For example, here is how the *Westminster Confession of Faith* (1647) summarizes the biblical elements of worship: "The reading of the Scriptures with godly fear, the sound preaching and conscionable hearing of the Word, in obedience unto God, with understanding, faith, and reverence, singing of psalms with grace in the heart; as also, the due administration and worthy receiving of the sacraments instituted by Christ, are all parts of the ordinary religious worship of God" (21.5). Sections 21.3–4 explain that prayer should also be a regular part of the church gathering (https://opc.org/wcf.html).

Finally, *circumstances* are the practical aspects of how a church organizes its worship gathering: when and where we meet, the layout of the chairs, whether we use air conditioning or not. Such questions are issues of prudence, not biblical requirement.[4] The regulative principle simply isn't about questions like whether we meet at morning or night, or whether we stand or sit.

Now, here's the thing: The separation between these terms—elements, forms, and circumstances—is admittedly a bit subjective. Over the centuries, Christians have disagreed on what is an element and what is a form. I might say that singing is an *element*, and that the question of whether we should accompany our songs with instruments is a question about *form*. But others have contended that the use of instruments is itself an *element*.

My intent here isn't to solve those debates. Rather, I wish to maintain that the regulative principle is still useful.[5] The regulative principle is a posture, as I said earlier. It's a way of

---

[4] See the *Westminster Confession of Faith* 1.6: "The whole counsel of God concerning all things necessary for his own glory, man's salvation, faith and life, is either expressly set down in Scripture, or by good and necessary consequence may be deduced from Scripture: unto which nothing at any time is to be added, whether by new revelations of the Spirit, or traditions of men. Nevertheless we acknowledge the inward illumination of the Spirit of God to be necessary for the saving understanding of such things as are revealed in the Word; and that there are *some circumstances concerning the worship of God, and government of the church, common to human actions and societies, which are to be ordered by the light of nature, and Christian prudence*, according to the general rules of the Word, which are always to be observed" (https://opc.org/wcf.html [emphasis mine]).

[5] Hughes Oliphant Old offers this excellent counsel: "The basic acts of worship [elements] we perform because they are clearly commanded in Scripture. The ways and means of doing them [forms] we try to order according to scriptural principles. When something is not specifically commanded, prescribed, or directed, or when there is no scriptural example to guide us in how we are to perform some particular aspect of worship, we should try nevertheless to be guided by scriptural principles" (*Worship: Reformed according to Scripture* [Louisville: Westminster John Knox, 2002], 172).

committing to conform our public worship to God's stated will as closely as we can, which is something I hope every Christian wants to do. So we aspire to make sure the elements of our public services are as biblical as possible, recognizing that this leaves freedom for us to adopt the forms of those elements that seem most wise and appropriate for our context.

Think back to the baseball umpire's manual. It regulates what a "pitch" is: where the pitcher must stand, what sort of ball he must use, where he can and cannot throw. A pitch is an "element" of the game. But a pitch comes in many "forms." Within the guidelines, pitchers have freedom regarding whether to throw a fastball, change-up, or curve; how to position their arm; where to aim the ball.

The regulative principle may not answer every single question we have about a worship service. That's not its purpose. Instead, its point is that when we sit down to decide what to do on Sunday morning, it isn't as if we're starting with a blank canvas. God has already written on that canvas, in permanent ink, the main strokes of how we are to engage with him corporately.

Simply put, the regulative principle keeps us from planning a service by asking, "What would we like to do?" or "What do we assume would 'reach' people?" Rather, it compels us to ask, "What has *God* called us to do?"

THE REGULATIVE PRINCIPLE SAFEGUARDS THE CHURCH'S LIBERTY

Amazingly, when we begin by asking that question—what has *God* called us to do?—planning a worship gathering is not stifling but liberating.

We know intuitively that it would be wrong to lead a church to say a prayer to a Hindu god, or to offer sacrifices to Baal. True believers should feel their consciences screaming at them *not* to worship in such ways. In Christ, we have been set free from such false worship.

But imagine being in the shoes of the Protestant Reformers. All your life, you've attended Roman Catholic masses in which the priest led you to pray to Mary and other saints, to make the sign of the cross, and to offer adoration to bread that had been "transubstantiated" into the physical body of Christ. These were all supposedly Christian acts of worship, yet many Reformers saw no basis for them in Scripture. They removed these elements from the public gatherings of their churches, and found their consciences wonderfully liberated.

Similarly, even if we are not reacting to a Roman Catholic context, we should likewise be concerned not to require our fellow church members to engage in something—as an *element of worship*—that may feel vaguely Christian-ish but has no backing in God's Word. For example, can we require them to watch an interpretive dance during church? To view a clip from a recent film?

It takes discernment to decide which of those sorts of things are "elements" or "forms," and which are allowable. I will leave them as open questions for now. The important thing is to remember that each member of our church has a conscience, a God-given sense of what is right and wrong. It is sin for a Christian to act against his or her conscience (Rom. 14:23). We must honor believers whose consciences differ from ours. As Paul says, "It is wrong for anyone to make another stumble by what he eats" (v. 20). Therefore, we shouldn't make another stumble by what we expect them to do in the corporate worship service.

Our consciences, of course, can be misinformed. A pastor should help his flock calibrate their consciences to align with Scripture.[6] This can get complicated fast. How can we preserve a clean conscience among our church members while not allowing them to play the "conscience card" on something that's merely a matter of preference? It requires pastoral judgment and sensitivity, but the basic answer is simple: by maintaining a clear biblical basis for each element of worship.

John Calvin stressed that what we do in a worship service is not neutral. The elements of worship either teach us about the God who is there, or about a god that we have re-made in our own image. That's why Calvin considered the Roman mass not just suboptimal but idolatrous to its core. It didn't represent the true God who saves through faith alone. He and other Reformers found it liberating to know that in every moment of a church service, we are doing exactly what God calls us to do.[7]

In other words, the regulative principle doesn't stifle. It frees. It liberates pastors from the tyranny of being clever or creative enough to attract people to the church. It liberates believers from having their consciences wrongly violated. It liberates us to focus on God, the source and object of our worship.

[6] For more, see Andrew David Naselli and J. D. Crowley, *Conscience: What It Is, How to Train It, and Loving Those Who Differ* (Wheaton, IL: Crossway, 2016).
[7] See Jonathan Gibson and Mark Earngey, "Worshiping in the Tradition: Principles from the Past for the Present," in *Reformation Worship: Liturgies from the Past for the Present* (Greensboro, NC: New Growth, 2018), 49.

Freedom does not mean doing whatever *we* want to do in church. It means resting in the joy that we are doing what *God* wants us to do.

THE REGULATIVE PRINCIPLE ORIENTS THE CHURCH TO LOVE

To put it another way, since the regulative principle protects freedom of conscience, it reinforces the corporate nature of the gathering. It orients church members to one another in love.

Romans 14 is a key chapter on giving up our rights for the sake of others. Christians may be free to eat meat sacrificed to idols, but "if your brother is grieved by what you eat, you are no longer walking in love" (14:15). Rather than insist on our rights, "let us pursue what makes for peace and for mutual upbuilding" (v. 19).

The regulative principle helps us apply this posture to the church's gathering. It may be okay for you to eat meat sacrificed to idols in the privacy of your home, but it is *not* okay to do so in the corporate gathering if there are believers there who would be "grieved" by it. Put simply, the regulative principle reframes our instincts about corporate worship. It undermines our individualism. It insists that we approach worship not asking the question, "What do *I* feel like doing to worship God," but rather, "How has God called *us* to worship him?" In other words, the regulative principle helps us put the "corporate" back into corporate worship. It safeguards our love.

C. S. Lewis famously said, "The perfect church service would be one we were almost unaware of; our attention would have been on God."[8] Derek Thomas, reflecting on that quote, writes, "That is what the regulative principle achieves for us in worship—a way of enabling us to be free from the whims of unwarranted structure so that our attention can be given to God."[9] I agree with Thomas. But I would add that the regulative principle also sets our attention on the bride of Christ. It awakens us to the church as a gathered, corporate body. It beckons us to prioritize love for others when we meet.

TEST CASES

Let's put the regulative principle to work. How does this posture toward Scripture help us where the rubber meets the road of planning a service? Let's try three case studies.

First, what about announcements? The Bible doesn't positively command us to have a section of our service for giving notices about items on the church calendar. Does that mean the regulative principle would forbid us from doing so? Not at all. We should conceive of announcements not as an element of the worship gathering, but rather as a circumstance of meeting together. A natural part of a gathering is informing the assembly about future meetings and other significant items of common interest. To be sure, announcements are sometimes given in a less-than-edifying manner, but the mere fact of including them does not undermine the regulative principle. Plus, Paul tells us that "all things should be done decently and

---

[8] C. S. Lewis, *Letters to Malcolm: Chiefly on Prayer* (New York: Harcourt, Brace & World, 1963), 4.
[9] Derek W. H. Thomas, "The Regulative Principle: Responding to Recent Criticism," in *Give Praise to God*, ed. Ryken et al., 93.

in order" (1 Cor. 14:40). He may not have had announcements in mind, but announcements certainly help us to fulfill this command.

Second, what about using drama in a church gathering? Many "seeker-sensitive" churches in the 1980s and '90s presented plays and skits in an attempt to engage with unbelieving visitors. But Scripture doesn't give us any commands to use theatrical arts in corporate worship or any narrative examples of such a practice. (Yes, Jeremiah and Ezekiel sometimes acted out illustrations of their messages, but these visual parables were directly commanded by God to depict his coming judgment—not exactly parallel to featuring a skit before a sermon.)

Some may maintain that drama is a *form* of teaching the Word, a creative way to convey truth through story and dialogue. Others, myself included, would argue that drama differs from teaching and preaching in significant ways. It tends to be more indirect and suggestive. With the exception of monologue, drama usually involves multiple actors and therefore multiple voices. Many people associate drama with entertainment; they treat it as a different sort of experience than listening to one person deliver a speech or lecture. These factors lead me to view drama as an *element* of worship, but one for which I do not see scriptural backing. And while previous generations of Christians don't hold authority over us, it's illuminating to observe that for centuries most Protestants have not recognized a biblical basis for using drama in worship services.

I don't expect these thoughts to convince you to stop using drama if you already do, although I hope they prompt you to reconsider. I'm merely illustrating how the regulative principle can and should shape the debate. It introduces the categories of liberty and love. Some believers may see drama as a *form* of teaching. But others argue that God has not called us in his Word to employ drama as an *element* when we gather corporately. If Scripture positively approved of drama, then we could use it to educate the consciences of those who disagree with using it in the gathering. But absent any biblical warrant for the practice, we shouldn't violate their consciences.

Third, what about baby dedications? This is a tricky one! You could make an argument for baby dedications as a *form* of prayer, since they usually involve praying for the child. I would observe, though, that a baby dedication feels a lot like a separate *element* of the service. The child is brought up front. The parents and congregation often say vows. It's a special event. To be honest, as a Baptist, a baby dedication seems to me like an infant baptism without the water. It's a ceremony, a ritual with its own choreography. Now, don't get me wrong: I love babies, and I love the intention behind baby dedications! But if the point is to pray for the new children of the congregation, I would suggest that churches should do just that. Pray for babies, but don't perform a special ceremony that might violate the consciences of believers who see no valid basis for such a practice in Scripture.

Again, I'm not expecting to persuade advocates of baby dedications to change their position here and now. I simply want to encourage us to frame our disagreements on such matters according to the central question, *How does God in his Word call us to worship him corporately?*

Even as we appeal to Scripture, different congregations will come to different conclusions. Notice how many times in the paragraphs above I used words like "feels" and "seems" in reference to determining if something is an element or a form. This is one of a thousand reasons why a church needs godly elders to exercise wise leadership. Various congregations may not always agree on how to apply the Bible, but we must agree to treat it as our authoritative and sufficient guide. We must seek clear scriptural warrant for every element of worship, and scriptural wisdom for the forms those elements take, even if that makes our church seem out of touch or outside the mainstream. When planning the corporate gathering, we take our cues not from culture, or from business manuals, or from so-called "successful" churches, but from God's Word alone. That's what it means to follow the regulative principle.

You won't find many baseball fans asking their favorite player to sign an umpire's manual. That's because the regulations aren't the point; the game is. The regulations only safeguard the beauty and integrity of the game.

Likewise, the regulative principle isn't an end in itself. It points beyond, to the God who has revealed how we should worship him. It points us to the people God has redeemed, reminding us that God is glorified when we lay down our preferences and freedoms to worship him as a united whole.

5

HOW SHOULD WE
ORDER THE GATHERING?

Your stomach rumbles. You pull into a parking lot and follow the *DRIVE-THRU* signs. Your mouth waters as you view high-definition photos of burgers and fries. You roll down your window. A voice crackles through a speaker: "Welcome to [insert your favorite fast food chain]. May I take your order?" You ask for combo #7. Right on cue, the car in front of you moves ahead. You inch forward and wait precisely 52 seconds. A clerk emerges from the window and announces, "Your total is $6.99." You hand him your credit card. He gives you a receipt, which you sign and return. You wait 14 more seconds. Finally, he places a warm paper bag in your hands. You close your window, unwrap your lunch, take a bite, and return to the road.

What I've described is a commonplace experience for millions. And yet it's also what we might call a "liturgy": a predictable pattern of steps, an everyday sort of ritual.[1] The

---

[1] For the notion of secular, "everyday" liturgies, I am indebted to James K. A. Smith and his "liturgy" of the shopping mall, which is the inspiration for my own, knockoff, drive-

storyline of a drive-through experience, if I might put it that way, has a beginning, middle, and end. When we look closely, we find deep, even religious, undertones. It starts with hunger and desire. The pilgrim draws near, joining other cars in the same lane. The menu offers a tantalizing promise of satisfaction. The cashier speaks first, inviting the driver to order. But a sacrifice is necessary; no free lunch here. The traveler (worshiper?) must pay. We reach the climax of the drama when the food passes from restaurant to car. The story resolves in the joy of a hot meal. The clerk pronounces a benediction—"have a nice day"—and the driver departs in peace.

Before you accuse me of reading too much into such a mundane event, notice that the whole thing has a necessary order. You must choose a dish before you pay, and pay before you eat. There are arrows on the ground telling you the right direction to go through the process. Each step matters on its own. But the pattern—the way in which the steps fit together—shapes what the experience *is*.

Consider, too, that the "liturgy" of the drive-through both reflects and reinforces the values of our age. It teaches us to prize speed and efficiency, anonymity and convenience. It trains us to treat food as a product that emerges magically when purchased. A drive-through both showcases and perpetuates the reality that we are a culture of people "on the go."

Don't worry. My point here isn't to bash fast food. Rather, I want us to notice that the order in which we do things matters. It trains our hearts.

---

through analogy. See his *Desiring the Kingdom: Worship, Worldview, and Cultural Formation* (Grand Rapids, MI: Baker, 2009), 19–24.

WHAT IS LITURGY?

As we saw in the previous chapter, God governs what we should do when we meet as a church. His Word gives us authoritative, sufficient instruction on what acts of corporate worship are acceptable.

Now, we turn to consider the pattern in which we arrange the elements of corporate worship. Scripture calls us to do all things in the gathering "decently and in order" (1 Cor. 14:40). This chapter is about structuring that order wisely.

Many theologians have called the order of service a "liturgy." The Greek term *leitourgia* referred to work done for the good of the public. When used in the context of a church gathering, "liturgy" refers to the "work" or ministry of exaltation and edification for which God gathers his people—or better, that God himself performs in and through his people.

Let me disclose that I'm ambivalent about the word "liturgy." It's become trendy, and I'm not sure if writers who use it always mean the same thing. I usually prefer to speak of the "order of service." But for the sake of joining and hopefully contributing to the conversation, I'll use "liturgy" in this chapter. For me, liturgy refers to the order of the worship service, particularly how it reveals and reinforces the nature of the service itself.[2]

---

[2] I am not here dealing with the idea of the liturgical "calendar" or "year" that some traditions follow. I'm focusing on the liturgy of the Lord's Day gathering since the New Testament clearly expects believers to gather weekly. Space does not allow engagement with the arguments for and against the liturgical year, but I hold the view that the annual feasts and festivals of the old covenant have been fulfilled in Christ and that there is no New Testament basis for a yearlong calendar (see Rom. 14:5–6; Col. 2:16–17; see also

To be sure, some may associate the idea of liturgy with high-church formalism and rote tradition. But in reality, every church has a liturgy. No matter how simple or complex, how short or long, each church's order of service expresses a set of theological values. And in turn, the liturgy gradually inculcates those same values in the church's members.

LITURGY AS CORPORATE DISCIPLESHIP

We should see the church's worship service—the whole thing, not just the sermon—as a mass discipling activity. Mike Cosper says it well: "The gathering isn't simply a single spiritual discipline; it's a host of them. It's a way of taking the experiences of prayer and worship, which we so often compartmentalize and individualize, and unifying them in the life of the congregation."[3]

Since the gathering is such a powerful corporate discipling tool, we should treat liturgy with care. Here's how Bryan Chapell puts it:

> Whether one intends it or not, our worship patterns always communicate something. Even if one simply goes along with what is either historically accepted or currently preferred, an understanding of the gospel inevitably unfolds. If a leader sets aside time for Confession of Sin (whether by prayer, or by song, or by scripture reading), then something about the gospel gets communicated. If there is no Confession in the course of the service, then something else is commu-

---

Hughes Oliphant Old, *Worship: Reformed according to Scripture* (Louisville: Westminster John Knox, 2002), 164–165.

[3] Mike Cosper, *Rhythms of Grace: How the Church's Worship Tells the Story of the Gospel* (Wheaton, IL: Crossway, 2013), 149.

nicated—even though the message conveyed may not have been intended.[4]

Imagine a diamond ring. The order of a worship service acts like the prongs that hold up the gleaming jewel of the gospel. Our liturgy should support and undergird the message of God's grace in Christ that we proclaim. Ideally, like the best prongs, the liturgy is unobtrusive—it gets out of the way so that the gospel shines bright and unhindered. Conversely, a poor liturgy is like a set of prongs that overshadow the diamond. The gem may still be present, but it is obscured. If a church isn't careful, its order of service can muddle rather than highlight the good news.

TWO EXAMPLES

To see how this works in practice, imagine two different church gatherings. Each congregation is the same size. They use the same musical instruments: piano, guitar, bass, and hand drum. More importantly, they affirm the same basic theological beliefs. But their liturgies differ in consequential ways.

The first was typical at the church I served at in my early twenties. It's a common evangelical liturgy. It begins with an energetic gathering song. Next, a pastor welcomes the church and invites everyone to greet those sitting nearby. He then offers a brief prayer asking God to bless the meeting. After that, the band leads a "set" of three praise songs, often in a sequence moving from an upbeat song about God, to a medium-tempo

[4] Bryan Chapell, *Christ-Centered Worship: Letting the Gospel Shape Our Practice* (Grand Rapids, MI: Baker Academic, 2009), 18–19.

song reflecting on what God has done, and concluding with a slow song of adoration to God. The worship leader closes the set in prayer, echoing the words of the previous song. A video clip introduces the theme of the sermon. The pastor then steps up to a bar table, reads a text of Scripture, delivers his message, and prays. He invites the congregation to sing a closing song, after which he gives a benediction. The band launches into the chorus of the final song as folks get up and leave their seats.

The second gathering is a service at Igreja Presbiteriana Barra Funda (Barra Funda Presbyterian Church) in São Paulo, Brazil. An elder begins the service by reading a call to worship from 1 Peter 2:9–10. He then offers an opening prayer. The congregation sings the hymn "The Church's One Foundation" in Portuguese. Next comes a Scripture reading from Leviticus 26:1–13. The congregation sings a song entitled "Your People," and then a member leads a prayer of praise. Another song, "Across the Lands," follows. Then the pastor preaches from Acts 2:42–47. On this particular Sunday, the congregation reads their membership covenant aloud and sings the hymn "Wine and Bread" to prepare for the Lord's Supper. A pastor leads in a prayer of confession, then the church celebrates communion. Finally, the pastor offers an intercessory prayer before concluding the service with a benediction.

What do these different liturgies communicate? What values do they reveal?

Let's start with the second one. At Igreja Presbiteriana Barra Funda, the order of service intersperses Scripture readings, prayers, and songs, which allows these various elements to interpret and shed light on one another. Notice how the readings from 1 Peter 2 and Leviticus 26 focus on the people of God. The titles of the songs show the same theme. These hymns and texts were chosen to set up the sermon text from Acts 2, which describes the fellowship of the Jerusalem church. We can see from the different prayers that various parts of the service focus on praise, or confession, or petition. In sum, this liturgy deliberately guides the church through an engagement with God centered on his Word. God speaks to begin the gathering; his people respond in prayer and song. God speaks in other Scripture readings and in the sermon, and his people respond by celebrating the Lord's Supper and bringing their intercessions to him in another prayer.

Contrast the gathering at Barra Funda with the first order of service I mentioned. That liturgy isn't sinful or wrong per se. But I wouldn't classify it as wise, healthy, or commendable. It has at least four weaknesses.

First, this service—presumably unintentionally—divides worship through song and worship through sermon. In fact, people who attend services like this all too often describe the singing *as* the worship, as if the other parts of the service aren't also part of how we glorify God. The structure reinforces this misunderstanding. There's a staging change (from music stands to bar stool and table) and a video clip as a sort of liturgical buffer between the singing section and the sermon section, making them feel separate and disconnected.

Second, this liturgy begins with us speaking to God in song followed by him speaking to us. That order is confusing. God first reveals himself to us by his Word. As we saw earlier, God works in and through us in corporate worship. He empowers our response to him. So, although this service may be designed to appear casual and approachable, it ironically asks too much of congregants. It expects them to be ready to jump into energetic songs of praise without necessarily hearing a reminder of who God is and what he has done for us in Christ.

Third, this order of service leaves two of the most essential elements of corporate worship out to dry: prayer and Scripture reading. There is no other Scripture reading in the service, aside from what the pastor might read in his sermon. And the prayers serve as transitions, not as substantive elements of worship in their own right.

Fourth, aside from within the set of songs, the service doesn't develop any broader narrative or theme. There's no sense of movement from considering God's character to praise, or from hearing God's law to confession, or from meditating on the gospel to thanksgiving. The best meals come in multiple courses that build upon each other in succession. This meal, however, lacks such a deliberate progression. It feels like the burger and fries from a drive-through.

Look at the structure of your church's most recent gathering. What is the "story" that it tells through the arrangement of the various elements? Is it a story worth instilling in your congregation, week after week?

If the liturgy emphasizes God speaking in his Word and his people listening, it fosters a congregational attitude of submitting to Scripture. If the service includes substantive prayers of praise, confession, petition, and thanksgiving, it will both teach the congregants to pray and reinforce the church's identity as a people of prayer. If the liturgy regularly underscores the depths of our sin before exulting in the heights of God's love in Christ, it trains the congregation to value Jesus's sacrifice. If the liturgy makes the sermon central, it teaches the church to esteem preaching as vital to its life and health.

A WORD OF CAUTION

At this juncture, though, I need to add a warning. Some theologians and leaders seem to talk about liturgy as if it were the *primary* tool that will bring greater health to Christian churches. They treat liturgical reform as The Answer to any number of problems in evangelicalism today. The argument goes something like this: since the order of our worship shapes our desires, then getting liturgy right is the key for Christian formation and growth. Are believers materialistic? The pattern of the liturgy will train their hearts to desire God's kingdom more than this world. Are believers individualistic? Liturgy shapes their identity as part of the community of faith. Are believers unconcerned with justice? The right liturgy will awaken in them a passion for equity and righteousness. And so on.[5]

---

[5] Though there is much to commend the high view of liturgy James K. A. Smith offers in *Desiring the Kingdom*—so much so that I cited it positively earlier in this chapter—it is at this point that I have some hesitations with his approach in that book. Smith offers helpful insights on the formative power of liturgy, but he sometimes emphasizes so strongly how liturgy influences the habits of our hearts that the Spirit-empowered ministry of the Word seems overlooked. Liturgy is undoubtedly a powerful force to mold what we love; one of the strengths of Smith's book is how thoroughly he demonstrates that reality. But Smith's argument that "we worship before we know" (34) and that liturgy leads our hearts in a "precognitive education" (136) seems to risk obscuring the primacy of the Holy Spirit's supernatural work of changing the heart

I agree that liturgy is a powerful force to shape our hearts. That's why I have spent this chapter encouraging you to be as thoughtful as possible about the order of your church service. Liturgy provides a skeleton, and it matters to have a skeleton as strong and well connected as possible. But you need more than a skeleton to have a living, breathing body. The actual content of each element of the service matters more than the order in which they are arranged.

Recall the excellent order of service from Igreja Presbiteriana Barra Funda we surveyed earlier. What if the hymns were changed to songs that lack key truths about God's grace for us in Christ? What if the prayers and the sermon no longer had a distinctive evangelical message but instead obscured or even conflicted with the gospel? You'd still have the Scripture readings, yes. But other than those, the service would be devoid of truth. The Word of God might be read, but the gospel

through the verbal proclamation of the gospel. Yes, we are all worshiping creatures who are indelibly shaped by the various "liturgies" in which we daily participate. Only the Spirit gives new life, however, and he does so through the Word. "So faith comes from hearing, and hearing through the word of Christ" (Rom. 10:17). To be fair, Smith helpfully qualifies his argument when he notes that we should not reduce corporate worship to a liturgical "pedagogy of desire," since God actively speaks by his Spirit to the gathered church (150). My concern is that readers may come away from his book seeing liturgy as of *ultimate* importance, when it would be better to see liturgy as *penultimate*. It is a pastoral tool for corporate discipling that is secondary to, and should be used in service of, the ministry of the Word. Mark Earngey puts it well: "The primary source of theology for the Reformers was the Word of God. However, because the Reformers understood the important interplay between how worshipers pray (*lex orandi*) and how worshipers believe (*lex credendi*), they saw liturgy as a powerful means by which to communicate theology. . . . *The liturgies were soaked in Scripture, and thus they did not return void.* What they often did return were transformed congregations, confident in Christ and courageous in good works. Through the liturgies of the Reformation, evangelical doctrine was as much caught in public worship as it was taught in published writings" ("Soli Deo Gloria: The Reformation of Worship," in *Reformation Worship: Liturgies from the Past for the Present* [Greensboro, NC: New Growth, 2018], 26–27, emphasis mine).

would never be explained. What I've just described is the case in many mainline Protestant and Roman Catholic churches today. They serve a meal that may be artfully arranged, but the food on most of the plates fails to impart life and health.

To switch analogies, a liturgy is like a pipe through which the water of the gospel flows. Pipes matter. Indeed, although it's sometimes barely perceptible, the material of the pipe adds its own flavor to the water. But water quenches thirst. Water gives life. Better to have leaky pipes flowing with pure water than amazing pipes hooked up to an empty well. If we care more about the order of service than the content of each element of the service, we may ironically end up neglecting the proclamation of the gospel.

We should strive to fill our services with the life-giving water of the Word of God. The Word, rightly proclaimed— through Scripture and sermon, through song and prayer, illustrated through baptism and the Supper—is what gives life to the church (Rom. 10:17; Col. 1:5–6; James 1:18). Scripture insists that God enlivens the dead through the declaration of a verbal pronouncement—so much so that he called Ezekiel to preach to a valley of dry, dead bones (Ezekiel 37). Our liturgy will flavor how we understand the message, but ultimately it's the message itself that God uses to save and transform his people.

PATTERNS IN SCRIPTURE AND CHURCH HISTORY

With that in mind, let's return to the positive benefits of liturgy. What would it look like for your church to adopt an order of service that is both shaped by gospel themes *and* full of gospel content? Scripture doesn't prescribe an overarching Liturgy with an uppercase "L" that every church must follow. Each congregation gets to decide the most edifying way to install its pipes.

But good liturgies share some common biblical themes and trajectories. Even if the Bible doesn't give us a step-by-step order of service, it still teaches us about how God engages with his covenant people. Furthermore, several key texts in Scripture seem to have a liturgical shape. We would be wise to look for patterns and priorities in God's Word as we determine the structure of our gatherings.

Consider Adam in the garden of Eden. The first man was created to worship. Jonathan Gibson observes a threefold pattern in how God engaged with the first human worshiper. First, God spoke to Adam, instructing him about which fruit to enjoy and which fruit was forbidden (Gen. 2:16–17). (I would add that God also called Adam into relationship with the woman; as God's people together in his garden temple, their life would be one of corporate worship [2:18ff.].) Second, there is an implicit response on Adam and Eve's part: to trust God and follow his Word. Third, there's a "fellowship meal": if the man and woman were to walk in obedience, they would partake of the tree of life in unashamed communion with God and one another. It's subtle, but I think Gibson is right: in Eden we see an embryonic liturgy. (1) God calls his people to worship him by his Word; (2) they (should) respond in obedience; (3) God fellowships with them.[6]

---

[6] Jonathan Gibson, "Worship: On Earth as It Is in Heaven," in *Reformation Worship*, 3–4.

Of course, sin ruins this rosy picture. Throughout the Old Testament, God's people can approach him only through the provisions he makes to deal with their guilt and uncleanness.

Still, there is a recognizable shape to the way God meets with his people in the ensuing biblical narrative. We see this particularly at two central events: when God ratifies the covenant at Sinai (Exodus 19–24) and when God meets his people at the temple (2 Chronicles 5–7). These two occasions aren't identical, but they share a rough liturgical shape: (1) God gathers his people near his presence; (2) God cleanses his people through sacrifice; (3) God provides his people mediated access to him; (4) God speaks; (5) the people give offerings, praise God, and consecrate themselves to God's service; (6) the people enjoy a fellowship meal.[7] Notice that, with some elaboration, the Edenic pattern of call to worship, response, and fellowship persists. Gibson perceives a similar liturgical structure in the book of Revelation.[8]

What do we learn from these texts? We see that when God meets with his covenant people, he is the one who initiates. Observe too that sacrifice, cleansing, and priestly mediation feature prominently. Our worship today should therefore stress the centrality of Christ as our great high priest who has cleansed us by his blood. We also notice that our response is multifaceted: God's people present themselves to him through prayer, song, and offering. Finally, we see that worship culminates in fellowship between God and his people.

Of course, many believers over the years have noticed these themes in Scripture and have developed liturgies informed

---

[7] Gibson, "Worship: On Earth as It Is in Heaven," 6–8.

[8] Gibson, "Worship: On Earth as It Is in Heaven," 18.

by these patterns. For those who hold to Reformed theology, Hughes Oliphant Old rightly argues that we would do well to learn from our "liturgical tradition"—that is, to listen to the wisdom in the liturgies of our ancestors who, like us, sought to be faithful to Scripture.[9]

To that end, Bryan Chapell surveys several enduring liturgical forms from church history and summarizes the main movements they share in common:

1. Recognition of God's Character (Adoration)
2. Acknowledgement of Our Character (Confession)
3. Affirmation of Grace in Christ (Assurance)
4. Expression of Devotion (Thanksgiving)
5. Desire for Aid in Living for God (Petition and Intercession)
6. Acquiring Knowledge for Pleasing God (Instruction from God's Word)
7. Living unto God with His Blessing (Charge and Benediction)[10]

ONE MORE EXAMPLE LITURGY

The broad structure Chapell identifies is similar to the typical order of service we use in my congregation, Capitol Hill Baptist Church. The rhythms of this liturgy have ministered to my soul for ten years. So, as one final example of how liturgy shapes the life of the gathered church, let's walk through a normal Sunday morning meeting at CHBC.

Allow me to make a few disclaimers first. I hope that what's remarkable about this order of service is how unremarkable it

---

[9] Old, *Worship: Reformed according to Scripture*, 165ff.
[10] Chapell, *Christ-Centered Worship*, 100. This is a summary of what Chapell calls "Liturgies of the Word," which explains the omission of the Lord's Supper, though I would suggest that the Supper and the notion of enjoying fellowship with God and one another could be included in number seven.

is. This is plain vanilla Protestant stuff: no bells and whistles, no innovative flourishes. Informed by classic Reformed liturgies, it's an order of service that would have been widespread in Baptist churches centuries ago. It's flexible; we vary certain details from time to time. I trust its main contours are also simple and biblical enough to transfer to various cultural settings. Still, my point is not that you should imitate this liturgy exactly. Instead, I hope it motivates you to reflect, brainstorm, and consult other examples.[11]

As you'll see, the sermon takes the central place. We try to take the main theme of the sermon text and infuse it throughout the whole service, so that the songs, Scripture readings, and prayers anticipate the sermon and prepare our hearts for it.

Preparation Music

Before the service formally begins, the musicians sing a few hymns and invite the congregation to join in while they are taking their seats.

Welcome and Announcements

The service leader (an elder or staff member) greets the congregation, offers a word of welcome to visitors, and shares a few brief announcements. Rather than make this time of greeting perfunctory, the service leader crafts his remarks with the upcoming sermon theme in mind. This service leader will continue to serve as a liturgical "tour guide" through the rest of

---

[11] See the Appendix for an assortment of service orders from contemporary churches. Gibson and Earngey's *Reformation Worship* (see note 5, above) contains an expansive collection of sixteenth-century liturgies.

the gathering. Through brief yet meaningful transitions, he applies the theological glue that binds together the various elements of the service.[12]

Silence and Scriptural Call to Worship

After the announcements, the service leader invites the congregation to spend a moment in silence. What a powerful picture: a congregation of people who are usually busy and bustling, now hushed. We are waiting for God to speak. Week after week, this time of silence reminds us that we have nothing on our own to say to God. We were not seeking him. He must seek us, find us, reveal himself to us.

And he does. God's Word pierces through the silence. The service officially begins when the leader reads Scripture out loud. This Scriptural Call to Worship takes only a few seconds, but it's a powerful symbol of God's initiative. He calls the meeting to order.

Summation of Belief

After God calls us to engage with him, it's appropriate to consider who this God is. The next aspect of the service is often a brief, variable reading that serves as an encapsulation of our theology. Whether it is the Ten Commandments, the Lord's Prayer, or a historic confession such as the Apostles' or Nicene Creed, this reading summarizes the faith that we confess. This moment conveys that we are a church united by sound doctrine. (A creed, by the way, is a teaching tool. It is a form of teaching the Word. Reciting

---

[12] For more on the vital role of thoughtful transitions, see Chapell, *Christ-Centered Worship*, 203–213.

the historic creeds of the faith helps showcase our connectedness with generations of believers who have gone before us.)

Hymns of Praise

Next, since God has welcomed us to praise him and we have recounted who he is, we now offer adoration to the triune God. Here we sing one, two, or three hymns that focus on God's perfections and mighty deeds.

Prayer of Praise

Just as we glorified God in song, we now magnify him in prayer. An elder or another mature man who aspires to eldership leads a prayer, three to six minutes long, informed by the themes and priorities of the upcoming sermon text and laser-focused on declaring God's praises. One of the most notable things about this prayer is that it is *only* a prayer of praise—no confessions or petitions here. We think it is instructive to model prayer that is entirely focused on who God is and what he has done. We hope that this prayer, over time, forms us into a congregation that is more and more God-centered, united by a vision of God's grandeur.

Scripture Reading

The God whom we praise continues to address us in his Word. This Scripture reading—which may be corporate, responsive, or led by one reader—is from the opposite Testament from the sermon text. This way, we hear from both the Old and New Testaments each Sunday, which trains us to appreciate the unity of all Scripture. Often, this reading will confront us with the reality of our sinful state. The Word convicts us, not just individually but corporately, that we are a people who have fallen short and need a Savior.

Prayer of Confession and Scriptural Assurance of Pardon

It is appropriate, then, to respond to this portion of God's Word by admitting our sins and pleading for mercy. Using language that is both piercing yet generally applicable, the person leading in prayer spends several moments confessing specific examples of sin on behalf of the entire congregation. This prayer trains us to be a church that is honest and personally transparent about our rebellion.

Thankfully, though, confession is not the last word. After this sobering moment of remembering our guilt, the person who led in prayer reads a passage from Scripture that comforts us with God's grace in Christ.

Hymns of Response

We proceed to sing another one or two songs that normally center on Christ and his redemptive work for us. Often, these are the hymns the congregation sings most loudly. Since we've taken the time to consider the weight of our guilt, now we exult jubilantly that Jesus has borne the wrath we deserved.

Pastoral Prayer of Petition

The third major prayer in the service expresses our utter dependence on God. Led by the one who is preaching that Sunday, this prayer normally moves in concentric circles outward. It begins with prayer for the congregation as a whole and for a few church members by name. It moves to prayer for our city and country, following Paul's admonition to pray for those in various spheres of authority (1 Tim. 2:1–2). Then, it proceeds to intercession for the world, as we ask God to send his gospel to faraway lands and to strengthen persecuted brothers and sisters in all corners of the globe. This sort of prayer trains the church to recognize how small we are and how sovereign and sufficient God is. It fosters a global mindset among the congregation, cultivating a concern for the spread of the good news in places in which we may never set foot.

Hymn and Prayer of Thanks and Offering

In recognition that God delights to answer the sorts of prayers we just offered, we sing a song of thanksgiving. This hymn prepares us for the offering, in which we acknowledge that all we have comes from God and so we give back to him. The service leader introduces the offering with a brief prayer of thanks. This section of the service trains us, week after week, in the gratitude and generosity that should mark God's people.

Sermon

Next, we glorify God by hearing his Word declared and applied to the congregation. We agree with Luther: "The preaching and teaching of God's Word is the greatest and noblest part of any service."[13] The sermon is not a dry, merely intellectual event. It is a crucial means that the Holy Spirit uses to minister grace to the gathered congregation. He feeds, forms, and fills us as we feast on Christ in his Word.

---

[13] Martin Luther, "German Mass and Order of God's Service: Adopted in Wittenberg, 1526," in *Reformation Worship*, ed. Gibson and Earngey, 107.

Baptism and the Lord's Supper

We normally celebrate the ordinances monthly, the Lord's Supper on the first Sunday and baptisms on the third Sunday. We place them here in the liturgy because they encapsulate and reinforce the preached Word.

Hymn of Response, Benediction, and Silence for Reflection and Preparation

In conclusion, we join our voices in a song that aims to take the thrust of the sermon and drive it deep into our hearts.

The preacher pronounces a final benediction from Scripture. Just as God had the first word in the service, he has the last. It is God who blesses us and commissions us to scatter for his glory. Often, we use 2 Corinthians 13:14, a rich Trinitarian blessing: "The grace of the Lord Jesus Christ and the love of God and the fellowship of the Holy Spirit be with you all."

Finally, we spend another moment in silence to allow the congregation to reflect on the entire service. This is an opportunity to do final business with God, to relish the benediction that has just been read, and to prepare our hearts for the week ahead. Like the moment of silence before the service, this pause is a subtle sonic boundary that sets off the worship service from the lively conversation and fellowship to follow.

CONCLUSION

The liturgy I've just described isn't flashy. It doesn't hinge on creativity or slick production. I'd guess that most of our church members don't spend their time rigorously analyzing the order of service in their Sunday bulletin. They simply participate, focused on God and one another. Hopefully, like when I gaze at my wife's engagement ring, what they notice isn't the prongs of the liturgy but the diamond of the gospel.

Sunday after Sunday, we engage with God corporately in roughly the same pattern. Our liturgy may be unremarkable, but week after week, it shapes who we are as a church. It fixes us on the remarkable reality that God has redeemed us in Christ.

6

HOW DOES THE WHOLE CHURCH PARTICIPATE IN THE GATHERING?

We began this book by considering the corporate worship service from a 10,000-foot vantage point. In chapters 1–3, I argued that since the church *is* a gathering, meeting together is of the essence of congregational life. God is the one who gathers local churches by his grace. He assembles his people to exalt his name and edify one another, and by so doing, to evangelize the nations.

Then, in chapters 4 and 5, we zoomed in to look at what a Lord's Day gathering involves. We saw that God governs how a church engages with him by his all-sufficient Word. We considered how the shape of the service, over time, shapes the spiritual health of the congregation.

The common aim in all of this, of course, has been to illuminate that corporate worship is a corporate phenomenon through and through. When we approach the worship gathering with a "thick" view of the local church, it transforms how we understand what's happening on Sunday morning.

Now, in our final two chapters, let's zoom in even further. Since a worship meeting is an expression of the church's congregational life, what does that mean for each element of the service? No surprise: I want to show you that every moment of the gathering has a rich corporate dimension. In chapter 6, we'll walk through many of the key biblical acts of corporate worship—reading and preaching the Word, prayer, and the ordinances of baptism and the Lord's Supper. In chapter 7, we'll turn to singing and consider how churches can grow a culture of robust congregational participation.

For each aspect of the service, I'll begin with some theological observations. Then, I'll make several practical suggestions for how churches might highlight the corporate dimension of that particular act of worship. These suggestions aren't strict biblical requirements, but ideas for application. They are "forms" of the biblical "elements." Hopefully they reflect scriptural wisdom, but you can take them, leave them, or adjust them for your own context.

READING THE WORD

God creates and sanctifies his people by his Word. Paul instructs Timothy to "devote yourself to the public reading of Scripture" (1 Tim. 4:13). For Scripture reading to be "public," there must be an audience. It is edifying to read the Bible aloud when you're alone, but a different dynamic is at work when "two or three are gathered" in Jesus's name (Matt. 18:20).

The public reading of God's Word was to mark Israel throughout her history. We see the nation gather to hear God's law under Joshua (Josh. 8:33–35), Josiah (2 Chron.

34:30), and Ezra (Neh. 8:3). As God's covenant people, Israel was to assume a posture of listening to his Word and obeying it. After all, the law's foundational command begins, "*Hear*, O Israel*"* (Deut. 6:4).

Turning to the New Testament, Paul instructed the Colossians to have his letter "read among you" and to "have it also read in the church of the Laodiceans" (Col. 4:16). He charged the church at Thessalonica, "I put you under oath to have this letter read to all the brothers" (1 Thess. 5:27). The final book of the Bible even promises, "Blessed is the one who reads aloud the words of this prophecy, and blessed are those who hear" (Rev. 1:3).

There's a simple lesson we should take from these verses: God's Word unites God's people. Deep covenantal undertones accompany the reading of Scripture. God has chosen to speak to *his* people, those he calls by his own name. The simple act of listening to God's Word, with a shared commitment to believe and obey it, binds a church together.

Lisa stands at the podium, opens her Bible, and begins to read John chapter 1. Her Trinidadian accent invites me to consider afresh the wonders of these well-known verses. I notice Daniel listening intently, and I make a mental note to talk to him about this passage later. At lunch after the service, Rebecca, a new believer, asks me what "the Word became flesh" means. Do you see how hearing God's Word read bolsters a church's unity? Even if only one person reads the Scripture aloud, the point is that all 40, or 400, or 4,000 church members *hear* the same Word at the same time. The Word then goes to work in our relationships.

With all of this in mind, how can we highlight the corporate dimensions of reading Scripture when planning a service?

- Have the church read Scripture corporately. The congregation can read a whole passage aloud, or you can split it up so that a leader reads certain verses and the congregation responds. There's something powerful that happens when the members of a church hear one another's voices proclaiming truths they hold dear.
- Select people from the whole breadth of the congregation to read Scripture in the service. Young and old, men and women, with a variety of cultural backgrounds and accents. When all these members read from the same Bible, it highlights a church's oneness. To be sure, heralding Scripture out loud in an edifying way requires skill and preparation, but many members can do it well if you're willing to coach them.[1]
- Introduce readings by briefly connecting them to the life of the congregation. "Brothers and sisters, many in our church are dealing with sickness and aging bodies. So listen to this word of hope from 1 Corinthians 15 about the resurrected body that awaits." "Church family, pay attention to James's instruction in this passage, which teaches us to be a congregation that resists favoritism."

PREACHING THE WORD

Reading and preaching the Word are closely connected. Preaching is expounding and applying God's Word to God's people. Like the reading of Scripture, preaching is a corporate act.

---

[1] For an excellent guide to how to read Scripture aloud in a church service, see Tim Challies, "The Public Reading of Scripture" (November 30, 2011. https://www.challies.com/articles/the-public-reading-of-scripture/).

One man preaches, but the presence of the gathered church means that a sermon is a communal affair. It may be subtle, but the fact that the whole congregation is there to listen will in some way shape what the sermon is. It's not a radio transmission to random, nameless people, but an address to real, embodied members who are known to the preacher and to one another. (Many church traditions, of course, have a vibrant culture of speaking up, exclaiming, and shouting "amen" during the sermon—a wonderful example of congregational involvement!)

In the Pastoral Epistles, Paul presupposes that Timothy and Titus preach to their particular congregations: "As for the rich in this present age, charge *them* not to be haughty" (1 Tim. 6:17); "Remind *them* of these things, and charge *them* before God not to quarrel about words" (2 Tim. 2:14); "Remind *them* to be submissive to rulers and authorities, to be obedient, to be ready for every good work" (Titus 3:1). God's Word doesn't change, but each preacher must apply it to his particular congregation. In other words, pastors shouldn't preach generic Christian platitudes into the air. They should speak to their sheep, their people. A Sunday sermon shouldn't sound like a message given at a Christian conference—as wonderful as conference sermons might be. It should sound like a father speaking to kids he knows deeply.

The grandson of famous preacher G. Campbell Morgan once remarked, "I was present in a church when he rose to preach, the lights in the main sanctuary were dimmed. But Dr. Campbell Morgan stopped his sermon to say, 'Will the ushers be so good as to turn on those lights again? I have to see the faces of my congregation; indeed, they are generally a part of my notes.'"[2] Preaching is not a one-directional speech. Wise preachers don't stick too stubbornly to the manuscript. They "read" their congregation and tailor their exposition to the saints before them.

The sermon is congregational in another sense, too: the church bears responsibility for what they hear. False preachers gain a platform because congregants with "itching ears" tolerate and even recruit "teachers to suit their own passions" (2 Tim. 4:3). By continuing to listen, a church endorses what it hears. We must teach our members to imitate the Bereans, who searched the Scripture carefully to make sure they were hearing the truth (Acts 17:11). Paul warned the Christians in Galatia that they could not pass the blame if they accepted a different gospel (Gal. 1:6ff). They were accountable for the preaching they embraced.

So what might it look like to underscore in practice how the preaching of the Word is a congregational reality? Here are several ideas:

- Announce your sermon text ahead of time and encourage members to meditate on it in advance. Not only does this help them individually get more out of the sermon, it organizes the church together around the text. They will discuss it together and share questions about it throughout the week.
- Apply the sermon to the church as a whole, not just to the individual Christian life. "What this means for us, CHBC,

[2] Howard Moody Morgan, *In the Shadow of Grace: The Life and Meditations of G. Campbell Morgan* (Grand Rapids, MI: Baker Books, 2007), 116.

is that we are praying that God would make us a people who are hospitable." Along similar lines, as you preach, teach the church about the church's own theology and corporate life. "You may have noticed we give a lot of attention to church membership and discipline here. That's because we're trying to be faithful to what we see Jesus teaching in this passage."

- From time to time, name specific members who exemplify the point of your sermon, or who have helped you formulate a particular insight. This makes the sermon feel less like a lecture and more like an address to your own spiritual family.

- As you preach, provide suggestions for how members can discuss various points in the text over lunch together, or how they might pray together about something you mention. This way, even in the application you provide, you are subtly training the congregation not simply to listen to the sermon with their own life in mind, but to take what they've heard and leverage it for the spiritual good of other members.

- Consider having small groups discuss the sermon text either in advance of the message and/or after the message to focus on application. Either way, the sermon text "reverberates" throughout the congregation, providing fuel for members' discipling of one another.[3]

- Involve members in your sermon preparation. E-mail them a couple of paragraphs from your draft and ask for their feedback. Ask what questions they have about the text. Meet with several members to brainstorm application together, so that your application stays rooted in the lives of your people.

---

[3] For more on this theme, see Jonathan Leeman, *Word-Centered Church* (Chicago: Moody, 2017), 22–23, 159ff.

- Similarly, involve members in your feedback process. Provide ways for trusted, mature members to critique your sermon—and really listen to them. They will gain a greater sense of stewardship for the ministry of the Word in your church, and their comments will enhance your preaching over time.

PRAYER

Corporate prayer during the worship service both reflects and promotes a church's unity. Gathered before the throne of grace, a church expresses its dependence on God through prayer. Again, as with reading and preaching the Word, corporate prayer is a thoroughly congregational phenomenon, even if one person takes the lead. The whole church joins their hearts together to agree with the one leading, and expresses their agreement by saying "amen."[4]

Jesus taught us to pray in the first-person plural: "our Father . . . give us this day our daily bread . . . forgive us our debts" (Matt. 6:9–12). The early church devoted themselves to prayer (Acts 2:42) and "lifted their voices together to God" when facing persecution (Acts 4:24). Paul instructs that "in every place the men should pray, lifting holy hands without anger or quarreling" (1 Tim. 2:8). Note that in this verse, prayer requires reconciling with one another. A church committed to prayer is one that will work to root out division.

Tony LoMoriello was a deacon in the church I attended as a teenager. He was known for his thoughtful prayers. I still

---

[4] For an excellent overview of prayer in the corporate worship service, see John Onwuchekwa, *Prayer: How Praying Together Shapes the Church* (Wheaton, IL: Crossway, 2018), 77–90.

remember a prayer he offered before communion one Sunday. In it, he likened our sinful hearts to coal that gets transformed into sparkling, clear diamonds by God's grace in Christ. The church was quite moved, and many chatted afterwards about how Tony's prayer had encouraged them. All of that edification took place simply because Tony was given the time to offer a substantive prayer and because he prepared his prayer with the good of the body in mind.

How can pastors highlight the corporate dimension of prayer when the church meets for worship?

- Pray in the first person plural: "we," "us," "our." This conveys that the leader is praying on behalf of the whole congregation, and it helps members pray along.[5]
- Build an "amen" culture in your church. I recently visited a church where the pastor led wonderful prayers of praise and confession. After each one, he said "amen," but the church stayed silent. That's a missed opportunity. Though the Bible doesn't strictly require it (however, see Ps. 106:48), it seems like a no-brainer to teach your congregation to agree with the prayer by saying "amen" out loud along with the person leading. In this way, the whole congregation verbalizes its ownership of the prayer.
- Pray for real needs in the congregation. Get specific. Intercede for members by name.
- Confess sin in prayer on behalf of the whole congregation. What sorts of temptations particularly pull at many church members? What besetting sins need to be brought into the light? You want to steer away from highlighting

---

[5] For many other excellent practical considerations in how to lead in public prayer, see Brian Croft and Jason Adkins, *Gather God's People: Understand, Plan, and Lead Worship in Your Local Church* (Grand Rapids, MI: Zondervan, 2014), 89–95.

one member's sin in a corporate prayer—"We confess that Tom has been coveting Nick's car"—but confessing sin with some level of specificity helps make the prayer convicting: "We confess that many of us have coveted each other's cars, houses, and jobs."

- Give lay members opportunities to lead in prayer. Their prayers will be seasoned with the everyday realities of life.
- Consider holding a prayer meeting at some other time in the week, such as Sunday evening or Wednesday evening. A setting like this gives a wonderful opportunity to shape your church's culture. Use this time to prioritize prayer requests that relate to the life and ministry of the whole church: pray for your church's supported missionaries, for members to be faithful in evangelism, for the pulpit ministry, for single members and families to build deep relationships, for a culture of transparency where members open up about sin and struggles, for the church's witness of unity in diversity, for members to know Scripture and refer to it regularly in conversations with one another, and more. Such prayers are a double-edged sword. First, God delights to answer prayers that flow from biblical priorities. Second, when you pray for such requests week after week, you catechize the congregation in what it means to live together as a church.[6]

BAPTISM

When we turn to the ordinances of baptism and the Lord's Supper, we find that each is thick with corporate, congregational meaning. After all, they are signs and seals of the new covenant.

---

[6] For more on prayer's role in shaping a church's culture, see Mark Dever and Jamie Dunlop, *The Compelling Community: Where God's Power Makes a Church Attractive* (Wheaton, IL: Crossway, 2015), 105–116, especially pages 111–113.

To be identified with Christ in baptism is to be identified with his covenant people. To participate with Christ at his table is to fellowship with his body, the church. Theologians rightly tell us that baptism and the Supper "join [believers] more closely to each other, set them apart from the world, and witness to angels and their fellow human beings that they are the people of God, the church of Christ, the communion of the saints."[7]

Consider baptism. Baptism is the immersion in water of a believer, testifying that your sins are washed and you are united to Christ through repentance and faith. But it's not only that. As a symbol of union with Christ, baptism also signifies entrance into Christ's body, the church. Paul writes, "For in one Spirit we were all baptized into one body—Jews or Greeks, slaves or free—and all were made to drink of one Spirit" (1 Cor. 12:13).[8] The waters of baptism are thicker than blood, it has been said. The bond you share with other baptized believers in the body of Christ transcends the ties of biological family, ethnicity, and nationality.

We see baptism's corporate meaning, in part, by the simple fact that believers cannot baptize themselves. Jesus has commissioned us to make disciples, "baptizing them in the name of the Father and of the Son and of the Holy Spirit" (Matt. 28:19).

---

[7] Herman Bavinck, *Reformed Dogmatics, Volume 4: Holy Spirit, Church, and New Creation,* ed. John Bolt, trans. John Vriend (Grand Rapids, MI: Baker, 2008), 489–490.

[8] Even if Paul is using the notion of baptism in the Holy Spirit here to refer mainly to conversion, as some commentators suggest, I would maintain that the verse still implies that the ordinance of water baptism has a corporate dimension. For water baptism depicts nothing other than our conversion, and Paul's point is that those who have been baptized (by the Spirit) are one body. In other words, those who are converted (and, following the NT pattern, baptized in water) are the body of Christ.

In particular, a close study of Matthew's Gospel shows us that baptism is the responsibility of the local church. We see this in three textual connections between Matthew 18 and 28 involving heaven/earth, Jesus's name, and his presence. In Matthew 18, Jesus promises to *dwell* with those who gather in his *name*, bearing the keys to bind and loose on *earth* what is bound and loosed in *heaven*. In Matthew 28, he reminds his followers that he possesses "all authority in heaven and on earth," charges them to baptize people into the *name* of the Father, Son, and Spirit, and promises to *dwell* with them always. We should conclude that baptizing new disciples is an expression of the authority Jesus has delegated to the local church, the institution that represents his name and enjoys his authoritative presence.[9]

To put it another way, baptism is far more than a way to get your individual Christian life started with a splash. It is simultaneously a funeral and a wedding vow. Baptism represents the death of the sinful flesh, severing our allegiance to the kingdom of this world. On the other hand, it depicts our union to Christ and his people. Baptism is how the church says to the world, "This person is one of us."

Churches, then, should look for ways to emphasize the corporate dimensions of baptism. Here are some suggestions:

- Perform baptisms when the whole church is gathered. As Hughes Oliphant Old explains, the Protestant Reformer Martin Bucer insisted on this point:

---

[9] I recognize that this argument may be new for some readers and that I've made it here in a highly condensed form. For a thorough look at Matthew 16, 18, and 28, and a more detailed argument for baptism as an expression of the local church's kingdom authority, see Bobby Jamieson, *Going Public: Why Baptism Is Required for Church Membership* (Nashville: B&H Academic, 2015), 83–89.

> [He] was particularly concerned that baptism be per-
> formed as part of the regular worship of the Chris-
> tian congregation, rather than as a private service
> conducted for the family. Bucer understood bap-
> tism as the sacrament of our incorporation into the
> church, the body of Christ. If indeed this was the
> case, then the church should be assembled when
> baptism was celebrated.[10]

- If possible, try to incorporate baptism into the regular
  Sunday service. For churches that must baptize outside
  the church's usual meeting place, this may not work. But
  it seems ideal to connect baptism, a picture of new life
  through the gospel of Christ, to the proclamation of that
  gospel in the corporate worship gathering.
- Highlight how baptism involves union with Christ's people through your introductory remarks. "We're about to
  baptize Mary as a sign that she belongs to Christ and his
  church." "As we celebrate baptisms this morning, we are
  welcoming those being baptized into the fellowship of
  our congregation."
- Ask those being baptized to share a brief summary of how
  Christ converted them. This way, the whole church knows
  who they are and can welcome them.
- Provide a way for the whole congregation to recognize and
  celebrate the baptism. Perhaps offer a corporate prayer

---

[10] Hughes Oliphant Old, *Worship: Reformed according to Scripture* (Louisville: Westminster John Knox, 2002), 13. Of course, in missionary settings where there is not yet a church constituted, this isn't exactly possible. Such situations are reminiscent of Acts 8:26ff., where Philip baptizes the Ethiopian official by the side of the road; there was no church yet in Ethiopia. Other exceptions may exist, such as someone who becomes a Christian the day before a planned move to a locale where there is no church. Normally, though, since baptism is an ordinance of the local church and involves identifying with the local church, it should be performed when the church is gathered. For more on this point, see Jamieson, *Going Public*, 213–215.

for the baptized believer, and lead the church in a hearty round of applause when she emerges from the water.

- Keep baptism connected to church membership. Aside from exceptional cases, churches should not baptize someone unless that person will also be joining that specific church as a member.[11]

THE LORD'S SUPPER

Baptism is the sign of one's entry into the new covenant family of God; the Lord's Supper is the church's regular family meal. The cup we share is the new covenant in Christ's blood (Luke 22:20; 1 Cor. 11:25), and this covenant is corporate through and through. As the temple of God's Spirit (1 Cor. 3:16), the local church has fellowship with Christ *and with one another* when gathered at the table.

I often feel chills down my spine when the nine hundred or so members of CHBC all raise their cups in unison to drink during communion. I taste the grape juice, aware that the brothers and sisters who have covenanted to care for me are all meditating on Christ's sacrifice just as I am. What was bitter for our Savior is ever so sweet for us. We may use separate tiny plastic cups, but the synchronized act highlights that we drink from one spiritual cup. The Supper unites us.

Do you remember what was one of the things that Paul said was wrong with the church in Corinth? They neglected the corporate dimensions of the Lord's Supper. It seems the rich were communing separately from the poor. Some were get-

---

[11] For more on the connection between baptism and membership, see Jamieson, *Going Public*, 162–166.

ting drunk while others were going hungry (1 Cor. 11:21–22). They had divided the body that Christ died to unite (10:17), leading Paul to exclaim, "When you come together, it is not the Lord's supper that you eat" (11:20). He urges them to wait for one another when they come together, and by so doing to practice the Supper in a way that discerns the whole body of Christ (11:33, 29).

John Calvin gave an insightful meditation on these corporate dimensions of the Supper. It's worth quoting at length:

> As [the bread] is made of many grains so mixed together that one cannot be distinguished from another, so it is fitting that in the same way we should be joined and bound together by such great agreement of minds that no sort of disagreement or division may intrude. . . . We shall benefit very much from the Sacrament if this thought is impressed and engraved upon our minds: that none of the brethren can be injured, despised, rejected, abused, or in any way offended by us, without at the same time, injuring, despising, and abusing Christ by the wrongs we do; that we cannot disagree with our brethren without at the same time disagreeing with Christ; that we cannot love Christ without loving him in the brethren; that we ought to take the same care of our brethren's bodies as we take care of our own; for they are members of our body; and that, as no part of the body is touched by any feeling of pain which is not spread among all the rest, so we ought not to allow a brother to be affected by any evil, without being touched with compassion for him. Accordingly, Augustine with good reason frequently calls this Sacrament "the bond of love."[12]

---

[12] John Calvin, *Institutes of the Christian Religion,* ed. John T. McNeill, trans. Ford Lewis Battles (Louisville: Westminster John Knox, 1960), 4.17.38 (p. 1415).

I recognize that the Lord's Supper is an area where many churches already have deep-rooted theological commitments and long-standing practices. Still, it may be worth reflecting on whether there are ways you can more clearly emphasize the corporate dimensions of this ordinance. Some ideas:

- Exhort members to reconcile any divisions between one another in preparation for the Lord's Supper. Announce when the church plans to celebrate communion so that they can examine their relationships beforehand.
- If your church has a covenant, you can read it aloud before partaking. In this way, the members of the church can reaffirm the commitment they've made to care for one another before participating in the ordinance that so clearly depicts their unity.
- Sing a hymn together while the elements are being distributed and/or after the church has partaken.
- Consider passing out the elements and having the congregation wait so that everyone can partake at the same time. When congregants eat the bread or drink the cup individually, they tend to experience the Supper as mainly a time of personal examination and fellowship with Christ. Waiting to partake together reminds the church that communion is, in fact, communal.

CONCLUSION

In all these aspects of the service, when the body of Christ gathers, we serve one another. It is good and right for the elders to take the lead in preparing Scripture readings, sermons, prayers, and the administration of the ordinances. But all of these are ministries of the whole church. The various *some-*

bodies of the congregation unite into *one body* to receive and share the ministry of the Word, and the Spirit builds them up together into maturity.

Corporate worship is a foretaste of the new creation, where God's people will forever minister to one another in perfect love.[13] In each element of the service, we prepare one another for eternity.

And that eternity will be rich with the sound of singing. So it is to singing we now turn.

---

[13] See Jonathan Edwards's masterpiece of a sermon, "Heaven Is a World of Love," in *Works of Jonathan Edwards, Vol. 8: Ethical Writings*, ed. Paul Ramsay (New Haven, CT: Yale University Press, 1989), 366–397.

7

HOW DOES THE WHOLE CHURCH PARTICIPATE IN CONGREGATIONAL SINGING?

Sub-woofers boomed. Spotlights beamed. On a giant LED screen, one line of lyrics appeared. A singer lifted a microphone to his mouth. His well-trained and polished voice echoed throughout the auditorium, swelling over synthesizer chords. As I looked around, I noticed a few people singing enthusiastically, with hands raised and eyes closed. Most of them, though, stood awkwardly. Some were trying—unsuccessfully—to sing along with the syncopated rhythm. Others had decided just to listen. I could hear every instrument loud and clear through the massive array of speakers, but I couldn't make out the voices of the people around me.

A different Sunday, I found myself guest preaching at Kew Baptist Church in London, England. The congregation is made up of about twenty people. They filed into the modest chapel and passed around some photocopied song sheets. One member had recently started taking piano lessons so that she could accompany the singing. She played a simple introduction to the hymn "O the Deep, Deep Love of Jesus." All together, the twenty of us sang along. There was no sound system, no PowerPoint. But we could hear one another. The true and timeless words of the song strengthened my soul.

I assume that both of the churches I've just described care deeply about corporate worship through song. The first, though, had weak congregational participation in singing despite an elaborately crafted musical production. The second had little in the way of a music program, but the congregation still sang with vigor. Why? The difference doesn't boil down to style or instrumentation. I've attended some churches with a "traditional" style of music that sang vibrantly, but others where formal and obscure songs accompanied by an overpowering organ worked against the voices of the people. Likewise, though I've attended some churches with "contemporary" music that drowns out the congregation, like the one I described above, I've visited others where everyone sings along wholeheartedly.

How can we explain the difference, then? No surprise: I maintain that a deep understanding of the local church is often what's missing when churches don't sing. Whatever else may explain why some churches sing well and others don't, how we view the church is a vital part of the equation.

In our previous chapter, we explored the congregational dimensions of many elements in a church's gathering. Now, in our final chapter, it's time to put the "congregation" back into congregational singing. As Psalm 149:1 says, "Sing to the LORD a new song, his praise in the assembly of the godly!"

A quick disclaimer as we begin: corporate worship through song is a vast topic. I won't be able to answer every question or solve every debate. My goals are more modest: to consider the congregational dynamics of sung praise and to provide practical suggestions for how churches might bolster their corporate singing.

SINGING IS AN ACT OF LOVE

Paul tells the Ephesians, "Do not get drunk with wine, for that is debauchery, but be filled with the Spirit, addressing one another in psalms and hymns and spiritual songs, singing and making melody to the Lord with your heart, giving thanks always and for everything to God the Father in the name of our Lord Jesus Christ" (Eph. 5:18–20). God is the primary audience of our singing, but verse 19 points out that there is a secondary audience: one another. One chapter earlier, Paul urges believers to speak the truth *in love* to one another (Eph. 4:15). Singing is one way we do just that.

David Peterson puts it this way:

> The God-directed ministry of prayer or praise and the notion of edification are intimately linked in the New Testament. Even 'psalms and hymns and spiritual songs,' which are expressions of faith and thankfulness to God, are to be considered simultaneously as the means of teaching and admonishing one another.[1]

---

[1] David Peterson, *Engaging with God: A Biblical Theology of Worship* (Downers Grove, IL: IVP Academic, 1992), 221.

This means that singing is part of each member's ministry to the whole body. When you join a church, you join the choir. You become a steward for the spiritual vitality of the body, a stewardship you fulfill in part by opening your mouth in song.

The church member enduring persecution from his earthly family needs to hear his spiritual brothers and sisters sing, "Jesus, I my cross have taken, all to leave and follow Thee." The Christian burdened by shame needs to hear us exult, "My sin, not in part, but the whole, has been nailed to the cross, and I bear it no more!" Our weary hearts long to hear the gospel reverberate around us in surround sound. We hear the voices of our fellow church members, and remember that we're not in this alone. God has welcomed us into his family.

It is no surprise that the singing of the saints warms our hearts. God himself sings over those he redeems (Zeph. 3:17). He made us in his image. In some faint way, then, our singing reflects his own beauty, his generosity, his creativity. Jonathan Edwards imagined heaven as a place where God's people express "the inward concord and harmony and spiritual beauty of their souls by sweetly singing to each other."[2] When we show the love of Christ through congregational singing, we enjoy what could be called a "forehearing" of the new creation's soundtrack of praise.

Let's put this vision of congregational singing into practice by answering a few key questions.

---

[2] Jonathan Edwards, The "Miscellanies," in Works of Jonathan Edwards, Volume 13, The "Miscellanies," Entry Nos. a–z, aa–zz 1–500, ed. Harry S. Stout (New Haven, CT: Yale University Press, 1994), 332.

1. WHAT SONGS SHOULD CHURCHES SING?

We should sing *biblical truth*. Paul says, "Let the word of Christ dwell in you richly, teaching and admonishing one another in all wisdom, singing psalms and hymns and spiritual songs, with thankfulness in your hearts to God" (Col. 3:16). This means we should regularly sing the biblical Psalms (translated into your church's language). We should also sing other God-glorifying material, though it isn't clear to me if there is a firm distinction between "hymns" and "spiritual songs." The Greek term *hymnos* simply refers to a religious song. "Spiritual songs" would seem to refer to songs that express or reflect upon what the Holy Spirit has inspired in Scripture. Paul's point is that we should sing a variety of songs, all of which summarize and celebrate the "word of Christ," that is, the message of the gospel.

This means that singing is part of the ministry of God's Word. When a congregation verbalizes truth in song, the Holy Spirit unleashes the double-edged sword of Scripture in our midst. We teach one another that God is "holy, holy, holy." We sing to one another that he is "immortal, invisible, God only wise." As we do, we come both to treasure and to understand God more deeply. As new converts and mature saints harmonize together, the church becomes a seminary in which all of us are simultaneously professors and students.

Because of this, I'd argue that a church's elders should exercise oversight of song selection. Hymns are an extension of elders' teaching ministry—after all, the overseers are those the congregation recognizes as "able to teach" (1 Tim. 3:2). When considering a hymn that is true and biblical but was written by someone who holds to questionable or false theology, pastors should weigh whether including that author's work could be dangerous for their flock. If the hymn writer is deceased or not well known, then using the song may be less risky. There is no exact rule to follow in such situations, but it is an area that requires careful wisdom.

My elders have assigned the responsibility for song selection to our senior pastor. He plans a few months' worth of services at a time. Each week, the pastoral staff gathers to look at his rough draft for the upcoming Sunday and offer ideas for improvement. I recognize that in some churches a "worship leader" chooses the songs. Even if that is the case, I encourage pastors to oversee the process and have final veto power over the church's master song list. Pastors can collaborate with whoever shares musical responsibility, whether it be a worship leader, deacon of music, or choir director. But they shouldn't abdicate their responsibility of overseeing the church's teaching ministry, which includes song selection.

Choose songs that complement the theme of the whole service. Ideally, the hymns, prayers, and Scripture readings imprint a photo negative of the sermon on our hearts before the preacher steps into the pulpit. They "preach" the text in advance, even if it's subtle.

We should also sing hymns of *heart-stirring beauty.* Singing deep truth isn't at odds with expressing sincere emotion to God. Our hearts are frail and fallen, so we probably shouldn't expect a mountaintop high of exhilaration during congregational singing each week. However, if our singing never moves us to transcendent joy in the Savior, we should be concerned about our spiritual state. The point isn't so much the intensity of the emotional experience we have from week to week—we can leave that up to God. The point is that as we sing, we grow in knowing, trusting, and adoring the triune God who is worthy of our praise. Through our singing, we help others delight in him as well.

Lyrically, look for songs that express rich truths in moving poetry. Pick hymns of substance, the kind that seem more profound the more you get to know them. I'm not thinking only of long or dense songs, but of those that give expression to believers' greatest hopes, joys, and longings, whether in a simple chorus or in six verses. Is this subjective? Sure it is. But use theological discernment, common sense, and whatever you know about what makes for good poetry, and pick hymns that seem to have the strongest words possible for your church. Make sure that over time your congregation learns songs that cover all the main headings of systematic theology.

Musically, the tune should fit the meaning of the lyrics—or better, enhance it. By "tune" or "melody," I mean the sequence of musical notes in a particular order and rhythm, to which the words of the hymn are sung. Ideal congregational songs have beautiful, expressive melodies that are nevertheless easy to learn for people from various generations, cultures, and tastes. Not all music is created equal. I encourage pastors and song leaders to develop aesthetic good sense to discern which melodies best serve the edification of their particular congregation.[3]

---

[3] For an introduction to the study of "musical quality" and how to evaluate music in a pluralistic culture, see Harold M. Best, *Music through the Eyes of Faith* (New York: Harper-Collins, 1993), especially chapters 2 and 6.

We should sing both *old and new* hymns. Some songs have stood the test of time for good reason. Embracing the best works of prior eras displays our unity with the universal church throughout time. It's also humble: to discard the masterpieces of Luther, Watts, Wesley, Bonar, and others in favor of an exclusive diet of the latest stuff written in a Nashville recording studio would commit what C. S. Lewis once called "chronological snobbery."

At the same time, the wonders of Christ should give birth to new songs in every generation (see Pss. 40:3; 96:1; 98:1; 144:9; 149:1). While age-old songs keep the church deeply rooted, contemporary hymns feel more accessible to many and can thus promote enthusiastic engagement. Both have value. I'm excited to see what the Lord will do in today's "modern hymn" movement, which seeks to combine rich theology with fresh melodies.[4]

We should sing hymns that express *the whole range of the Christian life*. Of course, congregational singing should resound with joy in the risen and reigning Savior. But Christ has not yet returned. God's people still experience childlessness, cancer, cruelty, and calamity. The psalms of lament teach us that faith means not running from God in our suffering, but running to him—with our questions, pain, and all. Why would we not cast our cares on him through song? Wise pastoral care includes cultivating a repertoire of hymns that "miserable Christians" can sing.[5] Psalms that are hon-

---

[4] See, for example, the hymns by writers and groups such as Stuart Townend, Keith and Kristyn Getty, Sovereign Grace Music, Matt Boswell, Matt Papa, and CityAlight.

[5] Carl Trueman, "What Can Miserable Christians Sing?," in *The Wages of Spin: Critical Writings on Historical and Contemporary Evangelicalism* (Ross-Shire, UK: Christian Focus,

est about trials. Hymns in a minor key. Songs that ask, "How long, O Lord?"

In all of this, remember that the congregational dimension of corporate singing should shape our approach to picking songs. Think of a museum curator with a limited amount of space on the walls. She picks only the finest works of art. Likewise, believers have a limited capacity of songs they can internalize, deep down. Pastors must curate their church's canon of songs with care, since songs are one of our most vital means of mutual Word ministry. Luther intentionally kept his hymnal at Wittenberg on the short side because he valued quality over quantity.[6] We would do well to follow his example: sing only the best.

2. HOW SHOULD WE ACCOMPANY OUR SONGS?

The question of musical accompaniment has divided some churches. However, when we frame our conversation about corporate worship with an emphasis on the *corporate*, we can de-escalate many so-called "worship wars."

Here's what I mean: we should look for ways to undergird the notion that singing is a mutual ministry of love. We should promote the unity of the body. How do we do that?

First, prioritize the sound of the human voice. It is instructive that the New Testament doesn't command us to use any particular instruments. We're free to play instruments; the

---

2004), 157–163. Also available online at 9Marks.org. See also Mark Vroegop, *Dark Clouds, Deep Mercy: Discovering the Grace of Lament* (Wheaton, IL: Crossway, 2019).

[6] Robin A. Leaver, *The Whole Church Sings: Congregational Singing in Luther's Wittenberg* (Grand Rapids, MI: Eerdmans, 2017), 154.

priests played them at the Old Testament temple. But the New Testament instructs us simply to *sing*.

So, how should we conceive of the musicians' role? If we expect those up front mainly to inspire and amaze us, we'll structure our music with that goal in mind. On the other hand, if we treat musical and vocal accompaniment as a way to facilitate and enhance congregational singing, it keeps the focus in the right place. Church musicians aren't performers; they're servants. Their job is to accompany, elevate, and beautify the congregation's ministry of song.

Let me make what might seem like a radical suggestion. You might find that using fewer instruments and lowering their volume actually yields a *stronger* and *louder* culture of congregational singing. There was a huge, loud organ at my church for years. In the 1990s, the organist retired. They couldn't find anyone in DC who played the organ *and* believed in the Bible. So the organ went silent and they started accompanying the singing from a piano. All of the sudden, people began to hear one another sing—and they *liked it*, so they sang louder!

My hunch is that if the volume and complexity of the accompaniment make it hard for people to hear themselves sing, the music ironically de-incentivizes hearty participation. Many congregants, even subconsciously, will simply stop singing—or start half-heartedly singing—because they can't hear themselves or others. This occurs whether a church has an organ, an orchestra, or a modern rock band.

So, to foster a culture of congregational singing, consider using fewer instruments and turn down the instruments you do use. Musical complexity for congregational vitality—it's a good trade.[7] Of course, it may be possible to have both! My friend Drew Hodge at Desert Springs Church in Albuquerque, New Mexico, often leads singing with a full band. His skillful volunteers have created quite artful arrangements. Their music is far more complex than my church's. But Drew also insists that all the musicians serving up front must *sing along* while they play their instruments. This signals to the congregation that corporate singing is still the main thing going on, and their congregation sings with gusto.

Whether or not you decide to simplify your musical accompaniment, I encourage every church to sing a cappella regularly. Perhaps drop the instruments out on the last verse of a song, or do so for a whole song. This helps the congregation hear themselves and reminds them that the singing is mainly up to them. When the voices are the only thing happening, people step up to the plate and sing out.

One more thing, and I realize I'm getting deep into the weeds here. But singing a cappella with harmony parts is far

---

[7] What about texts like Psalm 150, where verse 5 reads, "Praise him with loud clashing cymbals!" Doesn't that disprove my suggestion? I'm not against cymbals, drums, or loud instruments. They can facilitate the singing of God's people in wonderful ways, and it's clear that the Levitical priests played cymbals (2 Chron. 29:25). That probably means, though, that most Israelites only heard these cymbals a few times a year, when they came to Jerusalem for the annual festivals. (Regardless of how often the cymbals were played, there was of course no electronic amplification, so these instruments would not have sounded too overpowering.) Scholars engage in lively debate about whether the Lord's Day gatherings of the New Testament church were mainly modeled after the sort of temple worship we see described in passages like Psalm 150 or if they took their pattern from the Jewish synagogue service, which was simpler and focused on reading God's Word, hearing a sermon, and singing Psalms a cappella. Either way, at the end of the day, the New Testament doesn't mention what instruments we should use, but it focuses on letting the Word dwell in us richly as we sing, and on addressing one another in song. From that fact, I conclude that the most outstanding thing about our corporate singing should be the vocal participation of the whole congregation. The questions of how many cymbals to use and how often they clash would seem to be left to Christian freedom and prudence.

better than singing a cappella in unison. This is one reason why I encourage churches to incorporate harmonies in any way they can—either through printed hymnals, song sheets, or even projector slides that include harmony notes. Even if as few as 5 or 10 percent of the congregation can sing the harmony notes, it adds a richness to the congregational singing that is simply sublime. For this to work, the musicians need to play chords and harmonies consistent with the parts that are written. If they rearrange the song so that the vocal harmonies clash, it will discourage people from singing the parts at all and render the whole effort useless.

Second, prioritize unity when considering musical style. Since one of the main purposes of corporate singing is to build others up, music gives us a wonderful opportunity to "count others more significant than [ourselves]" (Phil. 2:3). Before he calls the Colossians to let the Word of Christ dwell in them through singing (Col. 3:16), Paul instructs them to bear with one another, forgive one another, and to "put on love, which binds everything together in perfect harmony" (3:13–14). After all, the church is made up of Jew and Gentile, slave and free, barbarian and Scythian (3:11).

As a people reconciled to God and one another, we should showcase our peace when we gather to sing. Our love matters more than our preferences. Pastors, therefore, should teach members to engage with the singing whether or not a certain song is in their favorite style.[8] These days, we can all listen

---

[8] Scripture doesn't mandate any particular style of accompaniment. That doesn't mean that every musical subgenre is equally well suited to congregational singing. But it does mean that churches should be careful not to designate one particular musical expression as *the* most holy, spiritual, or legitimate—whether classical, contemporary "praise and

to our favorite music in headphones whenever we want. But when we gather on the Lord's Day, we can display that the bonds of Christ are stronger than shared cultural background or musical opinions.

I often teach our members that we want a church marked by diverse musical tastes. We want classical music fans *and* hip-hop fans, jazz fans *and* pop fans, folk fans *and* rock fans. Music is so often a badge of one's identity and subculture. So the church has an opportunity to provoke our unbelieving neighbors: why do such different people enjoy singing together so much? Remember: for every song that resonates with you musically, there are probably church members who are laying down their preferences for your sake!

So, how do we keep the focus on unity? It's not the only way, but one suggestion is to keep the musical accompaniment simple so that the words and melody are what stand out. At CHBC, we do this by using only a piano and acoustic guitar. In a strange sense, this means the musical accompaniment disappoints almost everyone! Some people would prefer a rock band, others an organ, others a folksy roots group, others an orchestra, others a modern gospel choir. Well, we don't do any of that. But it's intentional. We want people who prefer all those different types of music to be able to sing as one.

There's no such thing as a style-less church. Every church has a style, a musical home base of sorts, even if it's intentionally simple like ours. You can't avoid it. And this means that, all half-joking aside about how our music disappoints everyone,

worship," or something else. The vital question to ask is what form of music will best facilitate *congregational* singing for your particular church.

145

there are some who find our music more familiar, and others who really struggle with it. Simply acknowledging this reality goes a long way. We must thank those who make a more costly sacrifice to engage with the hymns. We should honor them for their Christ-like example of singing along even if the music feels farther from their comfort zone.

We should regularly consider if our church's musical approach is keeping the good of the whole body in mind. Mike Cosper suggests that we view musical style through the lens of hospitality: we shouldn't make stylistic changes to attract the masses, but there may be small adjustments we can make so that singing is more *hospitable* for a wide variety of members and visitors.[9]

Here's an example, probably an imperfect one. My congregation has a long history of singing classic hymns in a fairly traditional style. But we're right in the middle of Washington, DC, a major African-American cultural center. The church is 70 percent white, but one might say our musical home base sounds even whiter than that. To be sure, traditional black and traditional white churches often sing many of the same time-tested hymns, but churches like mine tend to accompany them with far less rhythm and soul!

[9] Mike Cosper, *Rhythms of Grace: How the Church's Worship Tells the Story of the Gospel* (Wheaton, IL: Crossway, 2013), 181. Sometimes church leaders consider musical changes in the name of outreach. While I appreciate the desire to reach unbelievers, I'd argue that musical style is a woefully inefficient tool to "attract" a different demographic to your church. If you're a traditional sort of congregation with choir and organ and you want fans of indie rock to darken your doors, it's probably *not* wise to have your organist imitate the style of Arcade Fire or Vampire Weekend. Your church, I trust, can offer a bright witness to the indie rock community if you praise Christ vibrantly and sincerely *in your own musical expression*. Pray that preaching of the gospel, and the community of love it engenders in the congregation, would be what draws unbelievers to consider Christ.

Aware of this reality, our pastor led us to start learning some excellent songs from the *African-American Heritage Hymnal*, such as "All My Help Comes from the Lord," "The Crown," "He's Done So Much for Me," "Lord, Keep Me Day by Day," and "Where Shall I Be?" The goal was not only to show hospitality to black members and visitors, but also to edify all our members by celebrating the richness of the African-American hymn tradition, recognizing God's abundant grace in the men and women who penned these songs. Still, as a group of mostly white musicians, we knew we shouldn't try to accompany these tunes exactly like our musical counterparts in black churches. In fact, we knew that even if we tried it would look and sound awkward at best and deeply insensitive at worst. So we sought to play them simply and modestly, aiming to preserve the basic feel of the song but without going "all out" or trying to be something musically that we're not.

Have we struck the right musical balance? I'm not sure. It is a work in progress. But many African-American members and visitors have thanked us for including these hymns, even as I am sure they are exhibiting Christ-like patience with us musicians as we get comfortable with the repertoire.

3. HOW CAN CHURCHES PROMOTE ROBUST SINGING?

It has often been said that there are no neutral choices in music ministry. Every decision we make will either help congregational singing or hinder it. With that in mind, let's close this chapter with several practical ways in which churches can maximize congregational singing:

1. Keep participatory singing your main diet. Performed or "special" music can be edifying, but the New Testament commands *all* believers to sing. My concern about songs presented from the front while most of the church sits and listens, at least in our cultural moment, is that this practice seems to train church members in a posture of passivity. It conveys an expectation that singing is meant to entertain us.[10]

2. Encourage singers and musicians to lead confidently. A common mistake I see is that vocalists don't use their body language to signal when the congregation should join in. One of the simplest ways to achieve a substantial improvement in your singing is to have the leaders make the entrance to each verse exceedingly obvious: Take a deep breath; make direct eye contact with the congregation, with an inviting nod to signal that you're about to begin singing; and convey the emotion of the upcoming verse with your eyes.

3. Make the layout and structure of each song easy to follow. Long introductions and wandering instrumental interludes force the congregation to stand around and wait, feeling uncertain about when to sing. Strive to keep musical transitions (sometimes called "links" or "turn-arounds") between verses brief; the goal of these sections is to give a clear and intuitive setup for the beginning of the next verse.

4. Pastors should take the lead in enthusiastic engagement. Scripture calls overseers to set an example for the flock (1 Pet. 5:3). If a pastor enters the sanctuary after the service has already started, reviews his sermon notes dur-

---

[10] To keep special music truly "special," consider limiting it to unique occasions such as evangelistic outreach events or non–Lord's Day services such as Good Friday or Christmas Eve.

ing the songs, or generally comes across as detached, his body language tells the whole church that singing really doesn't matter. On the other hand, if he sings with all his heart, the congregation will see robust singing as the norm.

5. Turn the lights up. This is an area of wisdom, not law, but bright stage lights with darkness in the sanctuary convey that what's going on is more like a concert than a family meeting.

6. Consider seating. Can you arrange the chairs or pews so that the people can better see and hear one another sing? If so, you'll be able to reinforce the corporate nature of sung worship.

7. Promote musical literacy. There are numerous creative ways churches can help their members understand music better, with the goal of improving congregational singing. Consider including the harmony notes so that people can try to learn them by following stronger singers in a nearby pew. Share your church's songs in an online playlist so folks can get to know them well. Provide song sheets that members can use at home in personal and family devotions. I know of a church that offers a monthly "singing school," where they teach the harmony parts to one hymn. This way, over the course of a year, those who attend the meetings learn twelve songs in harmony and grow in their musical understanding. Over time, this simple initiative helped the whole congregation sing more robustly.

SINGING AS A PILGRIM PEOPLE

I recently visited an unregistered church in Asia. The congregation sang with wonderful intensity and emotion. Yet they sang softly and stayed seated, worried that standing would make their voices carry too much. If they sang too loud, they feared the police would find them.

If your church meets in a context where you can sing as loud as possible without fear of arrest, why would you not take full advantage of that freedom? Still, whether we're in Asia or America, all of us sing as a pilgrim people. All of us sing hymns of yearning, melodies of exile, refrains that long for our heavenly home. Together as a church, we raise our voices in unison, knowing that one day the storms of darkness will end.

Our singing anticipates something else—another time and another place. Our singing is not yet what it one day will be. It offers a foretaste of the day when all of God's family will gather around the throne. On that day, we will gather alongside our brave brothers and sisters in the new heaven and new earth, where no power or principality will oppose them because King Jesus has won.

I'll bet they will sing their lungs out. The trumpet will sound, a new song will begin, and God's people from every tribe and tongue will lift up an anthem of praise that will echo on and on and on—into eternity.

CONCLUSION

God gathers us as his people. *Who* the church is (we could say *whose* it is) shapes *how* it worships. And corporate worship, in turn, shapes the church.

What's next? Perhaps this book has led you to think differently about the church, and therefore to think differently about corporate worship. If I've proven my thesis, that the nature of the local church shapes what gathered worship is, then hopefully you now see ecclesiology and doxology as more linked, more mutually reinforcing. You may be wondering what practical steps you can take to strengthen the corporate worship in your own congregation.

Here are some thoughts on how to apply this book:

1. STAY FOCUSED ON THE GOSPEL

In all our excitement about corporate worship, we must never lose sight of the reality that worship is all about Jesus Christ. God has reconciled us to himself through the sacrificial, substitutionary death and victorious resurrection of his Son. The Spirit has powerfully brought us from death to life through repentance and faith in Christ. This is why we worship.

Reforming corporate worship is a worthy goal. But it's worthy precisely because corporate worship involves the church,

Christ's bride, whom he has redeemed and cleansed through his atoning work. So don't try to change corporate worship in order to make your church seem hipper, smarter, or more profound. Do it because you love the church for which Christ died and you desire for the congregation to grow in holiness, maturity, and love. Do it because you want the whole church to adore and treasure the God of the gospel more deeply.

2. PRAY FOR A HEALTHIER CHURCH

The more mature the congregation, the better its corporate worship. Therefore, one way to see corporate worship improved to is to pray for health in other areas. Pray that the congregation would clearly understand conversion and be faithful in evangelism. Commit yourself to teaching on and then practicing meaningful membership and discipline. Pray for godly, qualified elders who will lead the church to foster a culture of deep discipling relationships.

3. ENCOURAGE THE ELDERS TO LEAD

Every aspect of the church's meeting teaches something. The elders should give some form of oversight to the corporate gathering because the congregation has recognized them as "able to teach" (1 Tim 3:2).

So, when it comes to making changes to the church's approach to worship, these changes normally need to come from the top. If you are an elder, consider how to use the authority God has given you, along with the other elders, to shepherd the congregation through the way you organize corporate worship.

This doesn't mean every elder needs to be equally involved in planning the gathering. One elder, particularly a staff pastor or the senior pastor, can take the lead. But the whole elder-ship should feel a sense of stewardship for the overall vision for the church's worship as well as the content of each Sunday gathering.

If you're not an elder, there's still much you can do. Pray for your pastors to have wisdom. Talk with them about what you have learned about corporate worship. (Far better, of course, to reference the Bible than this book!) If you're involved in any aspect of the service, do all that is appropriate within your role to reflect Scripture's priorities.

4. TEACH PATIENTLY, AND MAKE CHANGES GRADUALLY

Paul instructs Timothy to "reprove, rebuke, and exhort, with complete patience and teaching" (2 Tim. 4:2). People have strong opinions about what happens on Sundays. Sometimes they have developed their view through a lifetime of prayerful study. Other times, they simply have an intuitive sense about what makes corporate worship "good" or "bad"—a sense that may or may not be "good" or "bad." For all these reasons, it is imperative that pastors teach, teach, and teach some more before changing something so central to their congregation's weekly spiritual walk.

Consider using members' meetings, Sunday school classes, Bible studies, and sermon series to teach on corporate worship. Meet with key volunteers to read Scripture, talk, and pray.

In corporate worship, rarely does anything require a drastic, immediate fix. People normally grow over the course of months and years, not days and weeks. Unless it is absolutely necessary, do not give your people whiplash by radically re-configuring the corporate service all at once.

5. TRUST GOD'S SOVEREIGNTY

There is only one perfect worship assembly: around the throne of the Lamb. So, until we join that "yonder sacred throng," we will always be able to identify something about our church's gathering that could improve.

God calls us to trust him. Worship is his idea. He doesn't accept our corporate worship because we offer it perfectly. He hears our praise because we are united to his beloved Son. He is the one who works in us by his Spirit. In Christ, corporate worship is a gift he first gives to us, then receives from us. We should work to reform and deepen corporate worship, but do so while resting in his good purposes and timing.

God created us for his glory. He redeemed us for his glory. He made us his people for his glory. He gathers us for his glory. And one day—on *the* Lord's Day—he will gather the whole church together for the eternal assembly that forever enjoys his glory.

Appendix

SAMPLE ORDERS OF SERVICE

As you consider how to shape your church's gathering, it can be helpful to study examples from other theological traditions and diverse cultural settings. To that end, here are several modern-day orders of service from congregations around the globe. While they vary in structure, shape, and length, they all feature the Word prayed, read, sung, preached, and depicted in baptism and the Lord's Supper.

Freie Evangelische Gemeinde (Free Evangelical Church), Munich, Germany | February 3, 2019

- Welcome and Announcements
- Call to Worship
- Prayer of Praise
- Hymn: "Seht unsern Gott" ("Behold Our God")
- Offering
- Scripture Reading: Revelation 21:10–11 and 21:22–22:5
- Hymn: "Wenn nach der Erde Leid, Arbeit und Pein" ("After Earth's Suffering, Work and Pain")
- Pastoral Prayer
- Sermon: Isaiah 4:2–6

- Hymn: "Es kommt der Tag" ("There Is a Day")
- Lord's Supper:
  - Invitation and Instruction
  - Silence for Personal Reflection
  - Prayer of Confession
  - Hymn: "Es ist gut, an deinem Tisch zusammen zu sein" ("It Is Good to Gather at Your Table")"
  - Distribution of the Elements and Partaking Together
  - Open Prayer
  - Collection for Benevolence Fund
- Closing Hymn: "Die Gott lieben werden sein wie die Sonne" ("Those Who Love God Will Be Like the Sun")

Risen Christ Fellowship, Philadelphia, PA | January 5, 2020

- Prelude Hymn: "To the Praise of His Grace"
- Welcome and Announcements
- Call to Worship: Jeremiah 31:33–34
- Pastoral Prayer
- Hymn: "This Is Our God"
- Hymn: "Genuine Love"
- Hymn: "Praise the King Who Makes Us One"
- Scripture Reading: Revelation 8:1–13
- The Lord's Supper
  - Introductory Instructions
  - Distribution of the Elements and Partaking Together
- Hymn: "The Church's One Foundation"
- Sermon: Ephesians 4:1–3: "Strive for Unity"
- Closing Hymn: "Never Cease to Praise"
- Benediction

An Unregistered Baptist Church in a Large City in East Asia | January 5, 2020

- Welcome and Announcements

- Call to Worship: Psalm 118:24
- Hymn: "All Nations Worship You"
- Prayer of Praise
- Scripture Reading: Jeremiah 8:4–12
- Hymn: "I Am a Lost Sheep"
- Statement of Faith Article III: The Fall
- Hymn: "Almighty God"
- Scripture Reading: 2 Peter 2:1–10
- Pastoral Prayer of Petition
- Hymn: "The Lord Is Merciful and Kind"
- Offertory
- Prayer of Thanks
- Hymn: "Doxology"
- The Lord's Supper
- Sermon: Matthew 21:23–22:14
- Hymn: "Trust and Obey"
- Benediction

Shiloh Baptist Church, Orange Park, FL | January 19, 2020

- Prelude Hymn: "Give You Everything"
- Call to Worship: 1 Peter 2:4–6
- Hymn: "Cornerstone"
- Scripture Reading: 1 Peter 3:8–22
- Sanctity of Life Presentation
- Pastoral Prayer
- Baptism
- Pastoral Welcome
- Scripture Reading: Exodus 3:13–14
- Hymn: "God Is"
- Sermon: 1 Peter 3:15–16; "Witnessing to Your One"
- Hymn: "Come to the Altar"
- Scripture Reading: Acts 20:35
- Offering and Announcements
- Benediction

Igreja Presbiteriana Barra Funda (Barra Funda Presbyterian Church), São Paulo, Brazil | February 2, 2020

- Call to Worship: 1 Peter 2:9–10
- Prayer
- Hymn: "Da Igreja o Fundamento" ("The Church's One Foundation")
- Scripture Reading: Leviticus 26:1–13
- Hymn: "É o Teu Povo" ("Your People")
- Prayer of Praise
- Hymn: "Senhor e Salvador" ("Lord and Savior," a translation of the song "Across the Lands")
- Bible Exposition: Acts 2:42–47; "How to Continue"
- Reading of the Membership Covenant
- Hymn: "Vinho e Pão" ("Wine and Bread")
- Prayer of Confession
- The Lord's Supper
- Hymn: Final Stanza of Previous Hymn
- Intercessory Prayer
- Apostolic Blessing

Satya Vachan (True Word) Church, Lucknow, India | February 2, 2020

- Welcome and Call to Worship: Isaiah 43:14–21
- Hymn: "Behold, I Will Do a New Thing"
- Hymn: "I Come Near to You, Jesus Christ"
- Baptismal Testimonies
- Baptism
- Baptism Hymn: "I Have Received Jesus and Have Become a Child of God"
- Congregational Reading of Church Covenant
- Pastoral Prayer
- Communion Exhortation from John 1:12
- Celebration of Communion

- Offering
- Offering Hymn: "My Life Changed When I Found Christ"
- Prayer of Thanksgiving and Preparation for the Preaching of the Word
- Sermon: 1 Peter 3:1-6, "Submission and Trust in the Christian Home"
- Benediction

GENERAL INDEX

SCRIPTURE INDEX

9Marks
Building Healthy Churches

9Marks exists to equip church leaders with a biblical vision and practical resources for displaying God's glory to the nations through healthy churches.

To that end, we want to see churches characterized by these nine marks of health:

1. Expositional Preaching
2. Gospel Doctrine
3. A Biblical Understanding of Conversion and Evangelism
4. Biblical Church Membership
5. Biblical Church Discipline
6. A Biblical Concern for Discipleship and Growth
7. Biblical Church Leadership
8. A Biblical Understanding of the Practice of Prayer
9. A Biblical Understanding and Practice of Missions

Find all our Crossway titles
and other resources at
9Marks.org.